The Rubenstein Kiss

James Phillips is a writer and director. *The Rubenstein Kiss* is his first play. *The Little Fir Tree*, a fairy story inspired by Hans Christian Anderson, was commissioned by the Crucible Theatre, Sheffield, and opened in December 2004. As a director his productions include *Frankie and Johnny at the Claire de Lune* at the Sound Theatre, London, *The Little Fir Tree* and *Macbeth* at the Crucible Theatre, Sheffield, *Trettondagsafton* at Teatre Hogskolan in Stockholm, and *Observe the Sons of Ulster Marching Towards the Somme* at the Pleasance Theatre, London, a production for which he won an Invention and Innovation Award from NESTA, the National Endowment for Science, Technology and the Arts.

T0262459

James Phillips

The Rubenstein Kiss

Bloomsbury Methuen Drama
An imprint of Bloomsbury Publishing Plc

B L O O M S B U R Y
LONDON • NEW DELHI • NEW YORK • SYDNEY

Bloomsbury Methuen Drama
An imprint of Bloomsbury Publishing Plc

Imprint previously known as Methuen Drama

50 Bedford Square
London
WC1B 3DP
UK

1385 Broadway
New York
NY 10018
USA

www.bloomsbury.com

BLOOMSBURY, METHUEN DRAMA and the Diana logo are trademarks of Bloomsbury Publishing Plc

First published in 2005 by Methuen Publishing Limited

This adaptation © 2005 James Phillips

British Library Cataloguing-in-Publication Data
A catalogue record for this book is available from the British Library.

ISBN: PB: 978-0-4137-7565-8
ePDF: 978-1-4081-4180-9
ePUB: 978-1-4081-4181-6

Library of Congress Cataloging-in-Publication Data
A catalog record for this book is available from the Library of Congress.

Series: Modern Plays

For my mother

The Rubenstein Kiss was produced by Kim Poster for Stanhope Productions, Joseph Craig, Janet Robison and Sally Humphreys in association with the Hampstead Theatre, London, where it received its world premiere on 17 November 2005. The cast was as follows:

1942–1953

Jakob Rubenstein   Will Keen
Esther Rubenstein   Samantha Bond
David Girshfeld   Alan Cox
Rachel Liebermann   Emily Bruni
Paul Cranmer   Gary Kemp

1975

Matthew   Martin Hutson
Anna   Louisa Clein

Director   James Phillips
Designer   Liz Ascroft
Lighting Designer   Hartley T.A. Kemp
Sound Designer   Neil Alexander
Casting   Gillian Diamond

The Rubenstein Kiss

'The most ancient of all societies, and the only one
that is natural, is the family: and even so the children
remain attached to the father only so long as they
need him for their preservation. The family may
then be called the first model of political society:
the ruler corresponds to the father, and the people
to the children. The whole difference is that, in the
family the love of the father for his children repays him
for the care he takes of them.'

Jean-Jacques Rousseau
The Social Contract

Characters

1942–1953

Jakob Rubenstein
Esther Rubenstein
David Girshfeld
Rachel Liebermann
Paul Cranmer

1975

Matthew
Anna

In both periods the story takes place in and near to New York City.

The staging descriptions are deliberately sparse and are simply indications.

Act One

Scene One

1975.

New York. A nearly empty room in an art gallery. Exhibition: 'Icons and Images of the 1950s'. Photographs of Marilyn Monroe, James Dean and others.

Matthew *sits in front of the Rubenstein picture.*

Later **Anna** *enters. They've never met. She sits silently between* **Matthew** *and a photograph of Marilyn Monroe.*

Anna You know, I think this is the most beautiful photograph I've ever seen.

Matthew Excuse me?

Anna I don't mean the Marilyn. I'm not a bottle-blonde nostalgic.

Matthew Is that why people like Marilyn?

Anna Bottle-blonde nostalgia?

Matthew Yeah.

Anna Yeah. And troubled-life nostalgia. Our little problems. Their big ones.

Pause.

Anna You know Marilyn carried a photograph of Clark Gable around with her?

Matthew I didn't know that.

Anna She spent ten or so years with this photograph in her purse. Whenever she was asked who her father was she'd pull out Clark and point to him. 'This is Dad,' she'd say. She made up her dad.

Matthew Shc made up her dad? And people let her get away with this?

Anna   I guess they didn't know what to say.

Matthew   No . . . You know a lot about Marilyn for someone who's not a bottle-blonde nostalgic.

Anna   Maybe I'm a troubled-life nostalgic.

Matthew   Are you?

Anna   No.

Matthew   Good.

Pause.

Anna   I haven't told you the best bit yet. You want to hear it?

Matthew   OK.

Anna   They made a movie together. *The Misfits*. The movie was called *The Misfits*.

Matthew   OK.

Anna   Arthur Miller wrote it. Her husband at the time. The guy who wrote –

Matthew   I know who Arthur Miller is.

Anna   In the movie Gable and Marilyn are lovers. In real life Marilyn was sick and wanting to divorce. In the movie Gable's a cowboy. A modern cowboy. Catching mustangs which get made into cat food or something. So she got to meet her made-up Dad. But it was kind of tragic, 'cause it was the last movie either of them made. The day after filming Gable had a heart attack. He died. And we all know what happened to Marilyn. But if I was a troubled-life nostalgic I'd probably think it hurt her, meeting her made-up Dad and him dying on her. Made her think it was her fault.

Through her story **Anna** *has been rolling a cigarette.*

Matthew (*smiling*)   You know you can't smoke in here.

Anna   I know. I'll go outside, in a moment. When I've finished with you.

Matthew   OK. (*Watches her.*) But you weren't looking at that photograph.

Anna   No. The Marilyn picture is not the most beautiful thing I've ever seen. Otherwise I'd be a bottle-blonde –

Matthew   Which of course you're not.

Anna   No. I mean this one. The one you're looking at. The Rubenstein picture. Do you know the story?

Matthew   Well, they gave me this pamphlet thing.

Anna   Gimme. (*She takes the pamphlet. Reads.*) 'Jakob and Esther Rubenstein were arrested in 1950 for giving the secrets of the atomic bomb to the Soviet Union. They were convicted of espionage, and sentenced to death. Esther's brother, David Girshfeld, was a chief prosecution witness against them. Through the long course of their trial and subsequent appeals they maintained their innocence. The case became a cause célèbre throughout the liberal world. Their execution in the electric chair at Sing Sing Prison, New York, in 1953 is still viewed by many as one of the excesses of McCarthyism. This photograph, The Rubenstein Kiss, was taken in the back of a police van during their trial.' Well, there you go.

Pause.

Matthew   Do you usually start conversations like this?

Anna   Only in galleries. I think the quiet air does something to me.

Matthew   Well, I'm going to get out of here. Shout a bit.

Anna   Buy me coffee.

Matthew   OK.

Anna   It's the most erotic picture. The having-you-here-and-now of it. Passionate.

Matthew (*offhand*)   Maybe I'll get you a print.

Anna   Oh, I'd like that. Passion needs restrictions.

Matthew   That is troubled-life nostalgia.

Anna   What I mean is, they can't have had any time alone. Jakob and Esther. During the trial. All the people watching, and separate cells. So they get pushed into this police van and they're handcuffed, but finally, at that moment, they're close enough to touch. And they kiss like that, and feel the flashbulbs on their skin. The light of the flashes seen even behind their closed eyes. Maybe people say they were playing up for all the cameras –

Matthew   Who says that?

Anna   I don't know, some people'd say it, say that's what they were doing, playing for sympathy. I mean, they knew the cameras were there, right? But you know what I think? I think whatever they did wrong, Jakob and Esther, they wanted to fix something in time. What they thought about each other. The flashbulbs fixed it for them. The Rubenstein Kiss. They had to do it. A compulsion. I think that's erotic, I think that's beautiful.

Matthew (*with charm*)   They were innocent, you know. They did nothing wrong.

Anna   Were they? How do you know?

Matthew   I'm a law student. You make me remember reading about the case.

Anna   I teach history.

Matthew   Movie history?

Anna   Just regular history.

Scene Two

1942.

New York. Evening.

Jakob *and* **Esther***'s apartment, a housing project on the Lower East Side.*

Esther *is laying a tablecloth on the wooden table. At this point she is twenty-seven years old.*

She is singing to herself, an aria from an opera. She sings pretty well, for an amateur.

Her brother, **David Girshfeld***, enters. He is twenty years old.*

David   Is he back yet?

Esther   Not yet.

David   When will he be back?

Esther   Soon.

David   When did he say he'd be back?

Esther   Soon.

David   Because I'm going to go and get her now. And then I'm coming back with her. I just want to know if he'll be here.

Esther   He'll be here.

David   I just want him to meet her. Tonight. He hasn't met her yet.

Esther   He'll be here. He had someone important to meet, but he'll be back.

She continues to sing to herself and prepare the table. **David** *sits at the table.*

David   I used to like it better when you sang jazz.

Esther   You don't like opera?

David   Bourgeois.

Esther   Well, Jake doesn't mind.

David   I mind. It's in Italian. Fascist language.

Esther   What was the name of the song I used to sing, Doovey?

David   Which song?

Esther   You know which one. At the vaudeville nights. Say it.

David   I will not.

Esther   That's 'cause you can't . . . Go on, Doovey. You know I like it when you say it. For your sister.

David (*mispronouncing*)   'Ciribiribin'.

Esther *laughs.*

Esther (*slowly*)   'Ciribiribin'. Go and get your girl, Doovey.

David *walks towards the door.*

Esther   It makes you bigger inside, you know.

David   'Ciribiribin'?

Esther   Opera. We can be big inside. Working people. That's what Jakob would say.

David   Once you'd told him.

Esther   Go on.

David *leaves.* **Esther** *finishes laying the table. She likes her things. When she has finished, she sits down at the table and sings very quietly to herself. Her back is to the door. Later* **Jakob** *comes in, stands watching her. He is twenty-six years old.* **Jakob** *is a slender, spare man, in his speech caught often between awkwardness and eloquence, uneasy in his movements.* **Esther** *starts to sing louder. As* **Jakob** *moves towards her, she turns. She keeps singing, to him, as he kisses her. When the Rubensteins kiss or touch, they kiss like real people – not movie-kissing, but the intimacy of people who need to be touched or* *held or kissed, without vanity. I think it was a surprise to both of them that anyone would enjoy kissing them as much as they do each other.*

Jakob Where are they?

Esther On their way. David's nervous.

Jakob Because I'm late.

Esther Yes

Jakob I wanted to think a little.

Esther What did they say?

Jakob It was a he. He said that I've been noticed.

Esther When would it –

Jakob Soon. Now. With the war –

Pause.

Jakob Should I?

David *enters with* **Rachel**, *his fiancée. She is a pretty girl, seventeen years old.*

Esther Hello.

Rachel Hi, Esther.

David I met her on the street. She'd already started out. Rachel, I'd like you to meet Jakob Rubenstein. Jake, this is Rachel Liebermann.

Rachel I'm happy to meet you.

Esther Get your sweetheart a chair, David.

Jakob I've seen you around, Rachel. At meetings maybe?

Rachel Maybe, yes. I go to meetings.

David So we're going to be married soon. Before I'm drafted.

Jakob We have meetings here sometimes now. In the new apartment. You could come to meetings here.

David   That means he likes you already.

Esther   Have some juice, Rachel.

Rachel   What work are you in, Jakob? Are you in the war?

Esther   Aren't we all in the war now?

Jakob   I'm an engineer. The Army Signal Corps. A radio inspector. But not in uniform. A civilian.

Esther   Jakob has qualifications. With electronics.

Jakob (*shy*)   And bad health.

Esther   He travels throughout New York and New Jersey with his work.

David   You working tonight, Jakob?

Esther   Yeah Doovey, he was working tonight.

Rachel   Doovey?

Esther   You haven't heard that?

David   When I was a little kid I had trouble sometimes with words. Saying the words.

Esther   I called him Davey, when he was a baby.

David   So you see –

Rachel   Doovey. (*Considers.*) Doovey.

They laugh. **Jakob** *has drifted out of the conversation, trying to make a decision.*

Rachel   This is a good place you have here, Esther. Warm.

Esther   Thank you.

Rachel   I always wanted a place like this.

David   We can get a place like this. When we're married.

Rachel   You think?

David (*shy*)   Yeah, I think so.

Esther   When Jakob and I were first married we were in Brooklyn. Shared a kitchen with another couple. Tiny. It works out.

David   And, God, when we were kids. No heat then. No furniture.

Rachel   You think it'll work out?

Esther (*tender*)   Yeah.

Rachel   My father said that a lot, when we were kids. Said it would work out. When he had no job. No job for ten years. Used to say it sitting under the hanging light, and then look over at my mother sitting at the table, wait for her to say the same thing. Never did, though.

Jakob (*suddenly, from the margins of the room*)   It'll work out.

David   What, Jake?

Jakob   It'll work out. I promise that.

David (*smiling*)   You promise?

Jakob   Things will change for you. It won't be like the past.

Rachel   You think?

Jakob   That's what the Party's about. Nothing big or complicated, just a real simple thing. That if we do enough, each of us, things can get better.

Esther   They can get better.

Rachel   You believe that, David?

Jakob   You can choose a generous spirit, not a fighting one. Spirit of dignity. You know, for the last ten years that's what our fathers had taken away from them. Dignity. Nothing and no one to look out for them. No state to be father to them. The depression took away their dignity.

David (*quietly*)   Yeah, I believe that.

Jakob   And we can go beyond that. You know my mother can't read and write English. No time, after raising four children, to learn English. After thirty years in America.

Rachel (*wanting to join in*)   I read about that, a pamphlet, how we go past our parents, where we sorta kill their world, they used a long word, do you remember, David – ?

David   I don't remember words so well –

Rachel   – and I understood that, that's why the world should be different, 'cause I hate my parents' world, 'cause it never never worked out –

Jakob   You know, I don't hate it, Rachel. I sorta feel strong because of it.

Rachel   Strong?

Jakob   When I was a kid my father'd tell me stories about Poland. About his father's father, Elia Rubenstein, who made his money cutting down trees and floating them downriver to the sawmills. Stories my father had been told first hand by this Elia, who lived to be an old and respected man. About fighting off the wolves in the deep forest. God I loved to listen to my father's stories, about his roots –

Esther   A Jew has legs, not roots. That's what our mother would say, Doovey –

Jakob   – and you know, it's not that this Elia was a great man. Wasn't a big man. Elia was kinda lazy, kind of a theatrical man, man with a great strong speaking voice. Flamboyant. Should have been an actor, you know, but lazy in his work. Not the guy to have working next to you through a day. So one night, after Elia got drunk, his friends tied him to a pile of logs and floated him off down the river –

David   Kinda looks like a criminal family you've married into, Esther –

Jakob   – but according to my father, and this is the thing I always remembered when I was a kid, Elia Rubenstein still maintained that the best morning of his life was when he woke up far down the river, in the middle of the forest, and stood up on his little raft and sang a psalm to the morning air. He was happy with that, a man who had nothing but his hope. And you know what I love about that, what I think that hope was?

David What?

Jakob Hope for the future. Not just his, but for the people who comes after. For us.

Esther He was singing his hope –

Jakob Yeah, I think he was –

Rachel That's a nice story, Jakob –

Jakob Yeah? I always loved to think of it. 'Cause I think we build upwards from the people that come before, upwards like a pyramid. And you know, tonight I saw this guy and he told me something I hadn't thought about before.

Esther What?

Jakob That the Fascists are in that very same forest, now, in 1942, killing people who should be like our brothers. And we need to work to fight against that. We need to do almost anything to stop that.

David Who'd you meet tonight, Jake?

Esther It doesn't matter now, Doovey –

Jakob Yeah, we can talk about that another time. But that's what's happening now, in 1942. (*Beat.*) And the word is patricide, Doovey.

David Yeah, that's it.

Esther And fratricide is the word they say when you kill your brother.

David (*to Rachel*) You know, I think they don't notice that I got smart. I mean science-smart, not word-smart –

Rachel *laughs.*

Esther (*moved*) Jakob. That question you asked me earlier.

Jakob   Yeah?

Esther   I think, yes. (*Beat.*) And David, don't think I didn't hear you, Jakob started you to being smart.

David   Yeah it's true. When they were courting and Jake was working for his college degree he used to study at our apartment all the time –

Jakob   I had to study there. My father still thought I was going to be a rabbi –

David   – and he gave me books, and a chemistry set, which made me want to be a scientist –

Esther   My husband was like a brother to David –

David   – and maybe I won't be an inventor now, what with being in the war, but a good job still maybe, like a machinist or something. Hey, you know when Rachel's birthday is? It's the best bit. May first. A May Day baby.

Jakob   Miss May Day.

Rachel *blushes*.

Esther   You two. Now Rachel, I've got some patterns for dresses I've been saving for you. Wedding dresses. Come and see. Before we eat.

Rachel (*pleased*)   OK. Thank you. You're spoiling me.

David   We like you.

Jakob   You hear that, David? Wedding patterns.

David (*smiling*)   I hear it.

Jakob   Pretty serious moment.

David   Yeah.

Esther   Don't tease him.

Esther *and* **Rachel** *leave.* **David** *looks at* **Jakob**.

Jakob   She's a good girl, Doovey. I like her. You be good to her.

David Yeah.

Jakob A strong girl, too. (*Smiles.*) Which you need.

David I'll be good to her.

Jakob Your sister is the strongest woman I know. Like in '38 she gets fired for organising a strike – leading the women in lying down in front of the bosses' trucks, right in the middle of the road –

David *is smiling.*

Jakob You know this story?

David You tell it, Jake, time to time. (*Finishes the story.*) She files a complaint with the Labor Board, wins it, and straight out gets a new job.

Jakob (*smiling as well*) New job that pays double. Double. And that's before the war, before the jobs came back.

David I know.

Jakob That's a woman.

David Yeah.

Beat.

Jakob Be loyal to her, to what you believe.

David Loyalty's like love, in action. You know who said that?

Jakob No Doovey, I –

David You did. To me. When you told me you were going to marry my sister.

Jakob I don't remember.

David I do, I remember. And I will. To her, to what I believe.

Scene Three

1975.

Late the same night of the gallery meeting.

Matthew *sits alone at the wooden table in his apartment. He strokes the table.*

Matthew　You know, I hate the endings of stuff. I think if you were here you'd tell me that's why I can't sleep after nights like this. Good nights. I think that's what you'd say, that I'm not able to close my eyes on endings. That's your fault, you know. (*He smiles.*) But I hate endings. I do. Ever since I was a kid, you know, I'd leave ten pages of a book unread. Or read those ten first, in the store, before I'd decide to go to the counter. Just to check.

I don't know if you'd like that about me.

I think you'd like this girl. I don't know, but I think maybe. She's kinda pushy. Miss Talky-Talky. We had some beers. And we talked. She talked mostly, but me a little bit. And she has this hair, this fucking hair, that sort of holds the light. You know, she kept talking about the picture, on and on, which was a little weird. But we got on well and then, well, later she came back here, and then. You don't really need to know about that, though.

History. A history teacher. I couldn't find a way to tell her, father, that history, it's written on our bodies, on the things around us, written in code.

You see, I used to worry that because you and I have only ever had these sort of conversations, Dad, because I basically sort of had to make myself up, that I might do things which you'd think were mistakes. Things you'd have told me not to do. But I don't worry about that any more. I used to think that these conversations that you and I have, these sort of hymns to absence, they were the only place we could come together. But family's not like that. That's what I've been working out. You're in the roots of my hair I think, aren't you? In my eyelashes, along the lines in my skin. There's strength in that. For me, I mean. Like tonight, when sometimes I'd feel worried if I couldn't think of anything smart or cool to say after she said something. You know, something smart enough in the moment so that she'd like me. That's when I get the strength from you. That's when I see why it wasn't so hard to make a bit of a man of myself, on my own, 'cause actually I didn't have to do it. 'Cause I had the knowledge of you all along. The strength of you.

But anyhow, don't be mad that we got physical so quick, me and Anna. I like this girl. That's really what I wanted to tell you tonight. We sorta had the night, you know, night where you fall. And she likes you. Like I said, she loves the picture, Dad. She likes you both, I think.

Anna *enters, wearing one of* **Matthew**'s *shirts, something like that. She sits at the table.*

Matthew   I thought you were asleep.

Anna   I woke up. Was waiting for you to come back to bed. What're you doing?

Matthew   Just talking. (*Smiles.*) To myself.

Anna   You do that often?

Matthew   Some.

Anna   Well, you're a strange one, Matthew . . . Matthew what?

Matthew   Matthew Maddison.

Anna   Ah. Matthew Maddison. MM – like Mickey Mouse. You know in Mussolini's Italy Mickey was appropriated as a Fascist symbol?

Matthew   Mickey? Is that true?

Anna (*not sure*)   Yeah. Could be. Think I read it.

Matthew   History teacher. Jesus. There's juice on the side, Anna. Anna . . . what?

She pours juice.

Anna (*playful*)   You want my name now? What will you do with it? With my name? Will you keep it safe?

Matthew (*smiling*)   Yeah, I think so.

He catches her, kisses her.

Anna   You'll spill my juice –

Matthew   Whose juice?

Anna   My juice –

Matthew   Whose juice? –

Anna   Miss Anna Levi's juice.

She escapes, sits in a chair opposite, drinks her juice. Pause.

So why'd you choose law?

Matthew   Because music was too frivolous. (*He lights a cigarette.*)

Anna   You were in a band?

Matthew   No, no I went to college. Then I got away for a while. Europe. Travelled. France and Italy. But music was in my family.

Anna   You've done a lot of things.

Matthew   Tried a lot of things. Done pretty much nothing.

Anna   So why law?

Matthew   I guess law's a tool, a weapon. A weapon either way, good or bad. Law broke Nixon, in the end. Hoover twisted it, used it, fucked with it. Got power from it. It's the white cells in our blood, save us or kill us.

Pause.

Anna   You don't own much. Not much in your apartment. A table, a bed.

Matthew   I'm new back in the city. Haven't filled it yet.

Anna   Nice apartment. Sexy to be so empty. We could be anyone here.

Matthew   It was my family's place. A little while ago. Grandmother. She sold pretty much everything, most of the furniture, everything went, you know. Cleared it all out.

Anna   Family place, huh?

Matthew   Family man.

Anna (*doesn't want to talk about family*)   OK.

Matthew   You've got your eye on me. Don't think I can't see it. (*Beat.*) So why a history teacher?

Pause.

Anna   You know, I read there's a type of fish, a fish that swims in the deep black ocean. There's no light down there. So it's kind of hard, even to be a fish. But I read that this certain kind of fish has a light in it, flashing. When they try and find a mate, these stupid fish, what they do is, they look for another light just similar to theirs. That's how to find a partner in the deep ocean. And you make me think of that Matthew Mickey Mouse Maddison. You make me think we sort of correspond, even though you're a strange one. That's why I've got my eye on you.

Pause.

Matthew   And the history?

Anna   I was good at it at school. Had an aptitude. I liked it. History's why stuff happens like it happens.

Matthew   I never liked it at school. Never trusted it. And now I find out Mickey Mouse is a Fascist, so I guess I was right all along.

Pause.

When you sleep, you sleep like a child, all earnest and concentrated and far away. You know that?

Anna   No.

Matthew   Always wanted to be able to sleep easy, sleep well.

Anna   You find it hard?

Matthew   Yeah.

Anna   My father does, too.

Matthew   Doesn't bother me.

Pause.

Anna (*playful*)   So I look at you in your empty, sexy apartment and I think this is a guy who is self-sufficient, not scared, not lonesome. And you can have a bad time with a man who is self-sufficient. Man with no trust.

Matthew   Oh, I can trust, believe me, I can trust.

Anna (*smiling*)   Yeah?

Matthew   Yeah. And don't worry. I'm plenty weak. Plenty needy.

Anna   So what scares you, Mickey Mouse?

Matthew   Absence.

He lifts her onto the table. Undoes the buttons on her shirt with a deliberation of touch.

Act Two

Scene One

9 August 1945.

The Rubenstein apartment. Late afternoon.

Rachel *is sitting at the table, drinking coffee.*

Esther *enters behind her, from the bedroom, carrying washing.*
Rachel *looks up.*

Rachel   The newspaper says it will take a million men to invade Japan. They're sending troops from Europe now Germany's finished.

Pause. **Esther** *is folding clothes.*

Esther   You worried they'll send David?

Rachel   It's stupid, but yeah, I guess.

Esther   He won't be sent. He's not a soldier. Not really. What's being done in the desert matters too much.

Rachel   Because the thing is, I'm gonna be having a baby.

Esther   Does David know?

Rachel   Not yet. I want to be looking at his face when I tell him. Smiley is what I've got to calling him. Though he smiles most when he's nervy. Probably will be nervy when I tell him.

Esther   Ah, that's wonderful news.

Rachel (*smiling*)   Isn't it?

Esther *kisses her. Pause.*

Rachel   You really have a home here, Esther. Even when Jakob's not here you have a home, the both of you. It's a thing you can sense.

Esther   Can you?

Rachel   Sure. You know, a home is a place people want to go to, to be at. You know how much Doovey likes it when we're here.

Esther *sits down with her washing on her lap*.

Esther   That's a nice thing to say, Rachel.

Rachel   When I was a little girl I knew that was what I wanted, a home. The feeling of a place. A place of safety. That's what we all want. You understand? Place of safety.

Pause.

Esther   You know the first time I met Jake?

Rachel   No. I mean, Doovey must've told me but –

Esther   It was at a concert, a night I had to sing a song. You know I did that a lot before I was married? Songs, oftentimes in competitions. Made a little money, too. We were a family that's always singing. The Girshfelds. And when I was younger I loved it. You know, one night, because I was part of this union, I sang at the Carnegie Hall. I remember that night, smelling the crowd, perfumed people, thinking how a big crowd of people all together is like a big smelling animal. And then going out into the light and it was like the whole world was watching.

Rachel   Jakob saw you at the Carnegie Hall?

Esther (*laughs*)   No. But that was the last time I liked to sing in public. Last time I was sure how to be outgoing. No, I met Jakob Rubenstein some months after that, just before Christmas-time. And that night I was meant to sing a song. It was just a little place, working place, but ever since that night at the Carnegie when I went out and it seemed like the whole world was watching I'd started to be frightened to sing in front of people. Because my voice on that big night didn't feel big enough. So I was sitting in a room outside the hall where I was meant to be singing, thinking that I didn't want to go out and sing. And then this man came into the room, this tall and slim and altogether awkward man came in and he asked why it was I was sitting on my own and not outside with the rest of the people.

Rachel   That awkward man, that was Jakob?

Esther   Yeah, that was my husband. And he talked to me and I don't really remember what he said, but it was just the way he said it, that way of his, not fluent or grand but like he felt it, speaking sort of slow and thoughtful, like he knew it. I think he made it like a dare, like when you're a kid, like those people out there were daring me to see whether I was able to sing. And after we spoke I went and I sang.

Rachel   That's a nice story.

Esther   True story.

Rachel   And how is Jake doing?

Esther (*wary*)   Well. He's doing well.

Rachel   What'll he do now?

Esther   He's picking up a little work just now. Then he's going to start a business. Just something small. Manufacture. When the war's done. He has a plan.

Rachel   He has the money for that? To get somewhere?

Esther   You know that a man in Jakob's situation can get money.

Rachel   When he was fired from the Signals Corps, why was that?

Esther (*folding the last washing with care*)   You know why that was, Rachel.

Rachel   Because they found out about the Party? That he had been a member of the Party –

Esther   That's right –

Rachel   Just that he'd been a member of the Party and that he'd lied about it –

Esther   Yes –

Rachel   – because if it was something else you'd tell me,
wouldn't you, Esther? If there was another reason they
needed to get rid of him –

Esther   Now the war's nearly over, it's happening a lot,
suddenly they're thinking more about who was in the Party –

Rachel   – because you see that if it was the other reason,
the other reason why Jake got fired, you see that I'd need to
know, right?

Esther (*finally*)   If there was another reason, Rachel, Jake
would tell you himself. Tell you both.

Pause.

Now you want to help me fold this sheet?

Rachel   OK.

They stand and stretch out the sheet for folding. **Esther** *sings quietly
to herself, to fill the air. Duke Ellington.*

Esther (*sings*)
    'In a mellow tone
    Feeling fancy free
    And I'm not alone
    I've got company.'

Unseen by the women, **David** *now stands in the doorway. He is
dressed in uniform. He is older, has changed. He takes a step into the
room. He recognises the song.*

Esther (*sings*)
    'In a mellow tone
    That's the way to live
    If you mope and groan
    Something's gotta give.'

David *takes the song on. Like* **Esther**, *he sings pretty well. As he
starts to sing they turn and see him.*

David (*singing softly*)
    'Just go your way
    And laugh and play

There's joy unknown
In a mellow tone.'

Rachel   David!

David   You weren't at the apartment. I thought you'd be here.

He kisses his wife and then more tentatively his sister. Holds them in an awkward three-way embrace.

Rachel   I didn't know you were coming back.

David   Leave. A few days. A surprise.

Silence as **Rachel** *holds him.* **Esther** *walks away, sits at the table. Later* **David** *looks up, moves towards the table. There's something distracted about him.*

Esther   Let me look at you. Older, oh yes, we've made you older. You've been busy in the desert.

David   Yeah, we've been busy in the desert. (*To* **Rachel**.) Our father always used to ask, in despair, so when will you be a mensch? Well, here's the mensch.

Esther   So Rachel and I were just talking about homes, the beginning of homes.

David (*distracted*)   It'll be time to get started on that soon. Real soon. Is Jakob here?

Esther   And you know, Rachel, Doovey's going to be good when it comes to homes. When he was just a kid, just sixteen, wasn't it, he rewired a whole apartment block, flicked the switch, made the lights work –

Rachel   Jakob's not here David.

David   Where is he?

Esther   He'll be back later. Let me get you some coffee. Sit down, let's celebrate you being here.

David (*shrugging*)   I just guessed when people started to hear the news he might come back here.

He sits down.

Rachel   The news?

David   Yeah. Big news.

Rachel   What news?

David   That what they made, all those guys, what they made in the desert is done. Finished and used –

Esther   What do you mean?

David   I guess it's what we all made in the desert. I mean, not me, not me really, I didn't even see how important it was, not till Jakob told me, I was just a somebody who knew to do things, just a machinist, a guy who could use tools with exactness. Not an important man. And there were men of genius out there, in the desert. You'd see them sometimes, tired scruffy men on tottering legs, with all this possibility, this making, going on in their minds. They were makers more than scientists, makers out there in the desert. And now everybody knows what they made.

Jakob *enters. Stands in the doorway.* **David** *looks up at him. Pause.*

David   You heard the news?

Jakob   It's on the radio just now. Spoken about on the street.

Esther   What news?

Jakob   Hiroshima. Four days ago they say. And one more, yesterday. Nagasaki.

Esther   What is a Hiroshima?

David   A city.

Jakob   A city in Japan –

David   What we made in the desert – we used it. A bomb. A bomb to destroy a whole city, just like flicking a switch.

Rachel   It can really do that? They killed a whole city? They killed everybody?

Esther   You knew it, what they said, that it was the biggest thing ever –

David   One plane, one bomb, one city. Before we went on leave they told us that the first one had worked, that it had happened . . . They tested it, you know. July, in the desert.

Jakob *still stands close to the doorway.*

Rachel   You saw it?

David   We were allowed to watch. I didn't, though. I was asleep. It was a dawn test. Too early to get up, I thought.

Esther   That's my brother, a man who could sleep through the end of the world.

Jakob   You didn't see anything?

David   I woke up with the light of it, intensity of light, like turning on the sun. The sun turned on at Alamogordo. An unremarked place. And I was in my bed, in the barracks, a way away.

Rachel   The man who came to us when I was staying with you out there in the desert, that fat man, the man who came and waited and then came back again –

David   We'll talk about that another time –

Rachel   Jakob's friend, who was expected, who came to us, that's what he took isn't it – ?

David   Another time, Rachel –

Rachel   But David, don't you see we have to go through this now, it's dangerous not to think about it now, it affects our future, we all have to talk about –

David (*finally*)   Dammit Rachel, not now.

Pause. **Jakob** *feels the mutiny in the room, looks to control it.*

Jakob   Rachel.

Rachel   Yeah?

Jakob   Tell us that story, the one you told me the other day.

Rachel   Which story?

Jakob   About your friend Louise.

David   Rachel?

Jakob   We were talking about the German camps. The Jews of Poland, the Jews of Europe, gone. And then Rachel told me this story about her friend Louise who fell to her death aged eleven years.

Rachel   You remember, David, I told you, years ago, my friend Louise.

Jakob (*to* **David**)   Rachel and Louise used to play on the fire-stairs outside her friend's block. Always playing there. But the tenement was in a bad state of repair, wasn't it, not looked after because it was the poorer people that lived there. And one night there was an accident.

Rachel (*realising* **Jakob** *will tell the story if she doesn't*)   It was the railings, they gave way. There was two places you could sit on the outside stairs – if you wanted to be private and talk without the adults. You could sit with your back to the wall or your back to the railings. And sitting with your back to the wall was better because you could see down into the street, and it was warmer. The night of the accident I was sitting with my back to the wall, and Louise was leaning on the metal railings. At that moment she was talking loudly, with a gesture, like an actress –

Jakob   – and they gave way, the railings, they were loose, and gave way. But the next thing was the important thing, right, Rachel?

Rachel *is uneasy.* **David** *looks at her.*

David   What happened?

Rachel (*it's difficult for her*)   It was nothing, really, just that some days after . . . Louise's mother, she came to me. And I was just a little girl, but I remember how she asked me, in a simple voice, why it was that I had lived and Louise had died. And I tried to explain to her about the railings and the wall, and how we kinda took turns with where we sat, but she was hurting inside and I don't think she could listen to me at all –

David (*to* **Jakob**)   Why do you want to tell me this?

Jakob   Because we go on with living for a reason – us, the people that survive. And because we're the people that survive we're responsible to those that don't. You understand what I'm saying, David, you understand that? All the lost ones, whether it's the Jews of Europe or just a little girl who fell to her death aged eleven years because nobody would look after the place she lived in, we're responsible to those people. And we have to do the difficult stuff because of that, we have to make sacrifices ourselves, in our own lives, take risks, maybe even put ourselves in danger. You see that?

David   Sorta.

Jakob   That's what I believe. Even today of all days that's what I believe.

Rachel   Sometimes I don't know why you think it's your thing to do, Jakob.

Jakob   Because it's us that's left. Because somebody's got to stand up, to balance things together. And it's *our* thing to do.

Rachel   I guess I just think sometimes you should look after your own. Your family. The ones close to you.

Jakob   We are your family

Rachel   Families change. Families grow.

Jakob   We're responsible to the world out there is all I mean. Can't lie about that, even to make things easier for us.

Pause. **Rachel** *is silent.*

Esther   Well, the war's nearly done. What you going to do when you're out, David?

David   No plans yet. (*Looks to* **Rachel**.) Work, find work. Get a place, proper place.

Esther   Jakob has an idea.

Jakob (*surprised, they haven't discussed this*)   I'm going to start a little business, here in the city. Small-parts business.

Rachel (*arch*)   'Cause Jake can get money.

Esther   And Jake wanted to know whether you might want to be a partner. In the business.

David   Me and you as partners?

Esther   Full partners.

David   Me and you, Jakob?

Jakob   Well, we have some expertise, right, Doovey? You a man who worked with Oppenheimer.

David   That'd be a great thing. Heh Jake, that'd be a great thing. What'd you think, Rachel, a business partner!

Rachel   It'd make money, would it, this business – ?

Esther   It'd make money –

Rachel   – because, David, we need to be thinking about what's important to us now –

Jakob   We can make a little money I think –

Rachel (*a little angry*)   – because now's the time we need to think about –

David   A business partner –

Rachel (*louder*)   – getting things together. Thinking about the future. Getting a home. For our family.

David   Yeah, I know that.

Pause.

Strange coming back to the city. So busy after the desert. The sky out in the desert, that's a thing to see.

The atmosphere is still uncomfortable. **David** *is nervous and starts to smile to himself. Then he starts to sing, tries to bring a little fun into the room, pretending to be Ella Fitzgerald.*

David
'I have eyes for you to give you dirty looks.
I have words that do not come from children's books
There's a trick with a knife I'm learning to do
And ev'rything I've got belongs to you.'

Esther *starts to join in, laughing too. She knows the song, of course.*

Esther
'I've a powerful anaesthesia in my fist
And the perfect wrist to give your neck a twist
There are hammerlock holds
I've mastered a few,
And ev'rything I've got belongs to you.'

David *is beating a rhythm on the wooden table. Now* **Jakob** *starts to join in, singing with a bad and happy deep voice.*

Esther, **David** *and* **Jakob**
'I'll converse with you on politics at length
I'll protect you with my superhuman strength
If you're ever attacked I'll scream and say "Boo!"
And ev'rything I've got belongs to you.'

Only **Rachel** *is not singing.* **David** *see this and stops. The song ends.*

David   I think we should go back home now.

Esther   Yeah you two, go get reacquainted. Good night.

David   Good night.

They stand. **Esther** *embraces her brother.* **Rachel** *is silent.*

Jakob   Goodnight David. Goodnight.

They leave. **Jakob** *watches them to the door. Silence. He stands still in the doorway for a moment. He crosses to his wife, kisses her.*

Jakob   My own love.

Esther   You OK?

Jakob   Yeah.

Esther   They're gonna be all right. In their hearts, people know what is right to do.

Jakob   The business. It's good for Doovey to be involved. Good idea.

Esther   You don't mind?

Jakob   He's like my brother, you know that . . . It has advantages.

Esther   I know.

Jakob *leans back against the table.*

Jakob   I saw our friend today. Because of the dismissal I'm gonna be too known to be touched for a little while.

Esther   That's all right isn't it, Jake?

Jakob   Yeah.

Esther   Safe?

Jakob   Sure. It's just I find myself a little tired by that . . . without things to do, without a task. It wearies me a little. When there's such things to be done.

Esther   They will be done. Things will change. Time will show things like they really are.

Jakob   It's just . . . you can't stop believing, you know, you can't just let things go.

Esther   I know.

Jakob   And it's just I think sometimes, I mean I . . . I don't know. There's this guy I was working with. Good guy. But he had been involved with a woman who was not his wife. I'm kinda innocent about that stuff –

Esther (*smiling*)   Innocent about that, are you?

Jakob (*smiling*)   Yeah –

Esther   Good –

Jakob   But one day I asked him how he could do that, make sense of that, you know, just day to day, just to himself, just walking down the street. And he said it was like there were two lives for him, like he was two different people, and if he told his wife, he'd have to choose which of those people he was – and I realised I understood that, you know, those two lives?

Esther   I know.

Jakob   I understood that, like being two people, cut in two, but both people smaller.

Pause.

Ah, it's just I find myself weary without something important to do. It scares me to be weary.

Esther *puts her arms around her husband.*

Esther   Shush, oh my sweet man, shush, such a man of worry. My soldier of worry.

Jakob (*looking down at her, searching for the words*)   You know I couldn't be a man without you. Just with a tilt of your head, your smiling head, I know what to be. My little delight, my hope.

He kisses her, lifting her and leaning back over the wooden table.

Scene Two

1975.

Matthew's *apartment, two months later. Evening.*

Matthew *and* **Anna** *sit apart on the floor, surrounded by hundreds of pages of documents. They are reading silently.* **Anna** *looks up at* **Matthew***, watches him for a moment. He is engrossed.* **Anna** *looks back at her papers.*

Anna   This is an unbelievable thing.

Pause.

You read this one?

Matthew   Um?

Anna   You're reading the trial transcripts too, right?

Matthew   Yeah.

Anna   I'm reading Sarah Stampe.

Matthew (*without attention*)   OK.

Pause. He looks up.

What I don't get is how you have all this stuff, all these papers?

Anna   The Rubenstein Commission for Justice, the commission to reopen the case. I'm working for them a little. They dump thousands of documents on the volunteers. And now there's gonna be a huge press conference and a kind of rally, in a month. Famous people, movie stars, are gonna be there.

Matthew   I know.

Anna   Do you?

Matthew   I read it in the newspaper.

Anna   OK . . . I like a good rally.

Matthew   Yeah, I guessed that about you.

Pause. He starts to read again.

Anna   You know who Sarah Stampe is, right? Matthew.

Matthew (*reluctantly drawn away from his reading*)   Yeah. Sarah Stampe. Yeah. The spy's woman.

Anna   Sarah Stampe. The Commie Vamp.

Matthew   Yeah, OK. What about her?

Anna   She was called as a witness at the Rubenstein trial.

Matthew   I know.

Anna   She was an American, who was screwing a KGB agent in New York in the '40s. A guy called Valentin Geller. At the trial she claimed she took phone calls for an American working for the Russians known to her only as 'Jakob'. She was kind of a sensation. Sexy woman in court, you know?

Matthew   I heard that.

Anna   I always imagined her with bright red polish on her fingers and lipstick like blood, smoking French cigarettes in the courtroom –

Matthew   How long have you spent imagining her?

Anna   Oh, just a little while –

Matthew (*smiling*)   Strange thing to think about.

Anna   Yeah, but look at this.

Matthew   What is it?

Anna   She's talking about her lover, this Geller guy.

Grudgingly, **Matthew** *puts down the papers he has been reading. He sits next to her and looks at Sarah Stampe's testimony.*

Matthew   What's important about this?

Anna   It's just that she knew nothing about him.

Matthew (*reading to himself*)   OK. Attorney for the Rubensteins: 'Now you have told us about a man called Valentin Geller, who was earlier known to you as Joseph.'

Anna (*reading as Sarah Stampe*)   'Joseph was the name he used during our first meetings.'

Pause.

Matthew   Is this drama group?

Anna   Yeah, I'm Lee Strasberg, come on.

Matthew (*smiling*)   OK. 'But this man also used other names during the period of your intimacy?'

Anna   'Yes. When we first became intimate I knew him as Thomas.'

Matthew   'And how long did you know him by that name?'

Anna   You don't sound much like an attorney, which is ironic considering that you're gonna be an –

Matthew   I'm close enough to being an attorney to remind you that you're under oath, Miss Levi –

Anna   Miss Stampe. Miss Sarah Stampe. (*As Sarah.*) 'I knew him as Thomas for one year.'

Matthew   'And, asking for the indulgence of the court, how long was it before you knew him by his real name?'

Anna   'It was three years.'

Matthew   Jesus, three years, who is this woman – ?

Anna   Well that's what I meant. It was a confusion of names. That's what worries me, you know, that people fall in love with the lies first –

Matthew   That worries you?

Anna   Yeah.

Matthew   Don't let it. Not like that. Deep down what people want is to know what's true.

Anna   You think?

Matthew   It's what I want.

Anna   It is?

Matthew (*shrugs*)   Yeah.

Pause. **Anna** *is making a decision. She goes for it.*

Anna   You know there's this story about Arthur Miller –

Matthew   The bottle-blonde nostalgic –

Anna (*smiles*)   He wrote a play about the witch hunts in the seventeenth century, in Salem, about all the people who were killed there for things they never did –

Matthew   I know the story –

Anna   The lead part in the play is a guy called John Proctor, and he's accused of being a witch, and he's gonna be hanged. There's a scene right at the end, where the priest or whatever, tells him that if he admits that he's been working with the devil, and declares his guilt, then his life will be spared. And he can't do it because he can't sign his name over to a lie. Can't do it.

Matthew   Well, I understand that.

Anna   It's kind of the climax of the play. And, you know, one night when the actor pretending to be this guy Proctor made his speech about how he wouldn't give up his father's name to a lie, something amazing happened. The audience started to stand up, one by one, with their heads bowed. Just stood there, silent. And the actors only found out later that at that moment, that exact moment, the Rubensteins were being electrocuted in Sing Sing prison, and everyone in that audience believing they were innocent.

Matthew (*quietly*)   I didn't know that story.

Anna   It's just it makes me think, about names and everything, and that woman Sarah Stampe –

Matthew   Sarah Stampe – ?

Anna   Yeah and how she lived her life, how her lover made stuff up, that I should tell you about –

Matthew (*with a sudden snap of anger*)   Sarah Stampe? Sarah Stampe's a nothing next to those people, a day-to-day liar, just a woman looking for a rush.

Pause.

Anna (*shocked a little*)   No, no, I guess you're right. I guess she's not important.

Matthew   You want to know the moment that's important? This moment here. (*He gestures to the papers he has been reading.*) Everything comes from the moment the brother lied. You want to imagine a moment, imagine the moment when David Girshfeld takes the stand, and everybody's watching to see if a man is prepared to put his own family in the death house just to protect his own skin.

Anna   I've imagined that bit.

Matthew (*looking at the transcripts*)   Read this. This is what happened.

Anna (*reads*)   'The testimony of David Girshfeld.'

Matthew   Yeah. (*With feeling for the role.*) Attorney for the Rubensteins, 'You realise the possible penalty of death for espionage in this case?'

Anna   'Yes sir.'

Matthew   'That your sister and brother-in-law could be sentenced to death?'

Anna   'Yes.'

Matthew   'And it is your testimony that your brother was a Soviet agent?'

Anna   'Yes.'

Matthew   'And you have testified that Jakob Rubenstein was in possession of microfilm and photographic equipment and that it was concealed in various domestic areas around the Rubenstein apartment?'

Anna   'Yes.'

Matthew   'You are aware that no such material or place of concealment has ever been found?'

Anna   'Yes, sir.'

Matthew   'Are you aware that you are smiling?'

Anna   'Not very.' It's nerves.

Matthew   It's lies. 'Are you married, Mr Girshfeld?'

Anna   'Yes, sir.'

Matthew   'And you have a baby daughter?'

Anna   'Yes.'

Matthew   'It's also your testimony that when you were visited in the desert, your wife was with you?'

Anna   'Well, sort of.'

Matthew   'Was she or wasn't she?'

Anna   'She was in the next room.'

Matthew   'But she was aware of your meeting?'

Anna   'She was aware that I was meeting with a man Jakob had sent.'

Matthew   This is the bullshit centre of it. 'She was aware that you were meeting with a Soviet courier?'

He stands, the transcript in his hand, still reading from it, his feelings rising. He doesn't notice that **Anna** *cannot see the transcript, cannot read the responses she is giving to his cross-examination, that she knows the answers by heart.*

Anna   'Yes.'

Matthew   'Do you love your wife?'

Anna   'Oh God, yes.'

Matthew   'And do you love your baby daughter?'

Anna   'Yes.'

Matthew   'And the Government has offered you things in order to testify against your brother and your sister, in order to save your wife?'

Anna   'I don't know what they are offering me.'

Matthew   'But you're lying to us today because your love for your brother and sister is less important than your love for your wife?'

Anna (*standing, shaken*)   Jesus, Matthew.

Matthew (*still angry in the moment*)   What?

Anna   You're right, you'll be a good attorney.

Matthew   Well, we don't need to read any further –

Anna   Why not?

Matthew   Because after that he starts crying like a child and there's a recess. Don't you want to destroy these people? Fucking destroy them.

Silence. **Anna** *walks around the margins of the apartment, stretches, uneasy.*

Anna   Two months and still no new furniture. Nothing new yet. Mickey.

Matthew   You're new. (*Smiles.*) Newish. Thought you liked an empty place.

Anna   I liked it as a beginning.

Matthew   It's a good way to live. Always wanted a place without context.

Anna   I can see that about you. Is that why I don't meet your friends, your family? What are we, love affair without context?

Matthew   I'm new back in the city.

Anna   Not a pariah girlfriend, then?

Matthew   Maybe I like for things to be separate.

Anna (*hurt*)   OK.

Matthew   It bothers you.

She moves to him, kisses him hard.

Anna   Yeah, it bothers me. I should go. We could maybe talk another time.

Matthew   OK.

She moves for the door, still hurt.

Hey. It's OK.

She pauses.

It's all right. (*He starts to half-speak, half-sing. Joni Mitchell, 'A Case of You', been in his mind.*)

'Oh you are in my blood like holy wine
You taste so bitter and so sweet.'

Anna   Don't.

He goes to her, touches her face.

Matthew
'Oh I could drink a case of you
And I would still be on my feet.'

Anna (*quietly*)   I'll see you soon, yeah?

Matthew   Yeah.

She starts to gather up papers.

Hey, leave this stuff, would you? Just for a day or two. I'd like to look at it a little.

Anna   Yeah, OK.

She picks up her bag, leaves **Matthew** *surrounded by papers. He sits down amongst them.*

Matthew (*sings to himself*)
'I remember that time you told me, you said,
"Love is touching souls"
Surely you touched mine
'Cause part of you pours out of me
In these lines from time to time.'

Scene Three

New Year's Eve, 1950.

Late afternoon. The front room of the Girshfeld apartment, Lower East Side, New York. The apartment is much shabbier than where **Jakob** *and* **Esther** *live. Second-hand furniture, no steam heat, that kind of thing. There's some sense of enforced cheer: evidence of preparations for* *a party have been made, but done on the cheap.* **Jakob** *and* **Esther** *sit in the front room, slightly uncomfortable. Next to* **Jakob** *is a pram, which holds their baby son* **Matthew**. *Absent-mindedly* **Jakob** *touches the fabric, strokes it.*

Jakob   Should we be doing something? To help, I mean?

Esther   I'll go and check on them in a minute.

Pause.

Jakob   Were they arguing in there earlier?

Esther   I don't know.

Jakob   It's just that I thought I heard raised voices.

Esther   Jake, I don't know.

Pause.

Jakob   We were right to come early, see if we could help.

Esther   Yeah.

Jakob   And I need to speak to David alone.

Esther   I know.

Pause.

Jakob   Cold. (*He gestures to the apartment.*)

Esther   Yeah. I'm gonna see if I can help Rachel.

Jakob   OK.

Esther *leaves for the kitchen. After a moment* **Jakob** *sits on the arm of the chair, looks into the pram, smiles.*

Jakob   Hello, little man, sleepy little soldier. You OK in there? Now this is where your uncle and aunt live. David and Rachel. And they love you very much.

David *enters from the kitchen, tie undone. He looks tired.*

David   Hey Jake.

Jakob   Hey.

David *walks to the pram. He sits near it, looks in, on the opposite side to* **Jakob**.

David   Hey, little Matthew Rubenstein.

Jakob   I was telling him that he was at his uncle and aunt's.

David   Quiet little guy, isn't he?

Jakob   He's a good baby.

David   You wait, Jake, wait till he starts singing like his mother, without restraint. When she was a kid, God could she sing and how . . .

Jakob   I think he likes it here. At his uncle's.

David   I think he's probably cold here, like the rest of us. No central heating. The gas heater, the portable, it's in the kitchen, I put it on full-flame for Rachel.

Jakob   How is she?

David   A little . . . uptight, nervous. This pregnancy, it's got us both kinda nervous . . . you know – ?

Jakob   It's understandable –

David   – and for Rachel . . . it's hard . . . the baby born dead, that shouldn't happen to a woman . . .

Jakob   No . . . but to get pregnant again, that's a blessing.

David   Blessing . . . (*Smiles.*) religion's not very revolutionary.

Jakob (*smiles*)   Old habit, my first passion.

Beat.

Jakob (*to the baby*)   And look how happy little Matthew is here.

David   Then he's pretty much the only one.

Beat.

You know what I'm thinking about?

Jakob   No.

David   Fourteen dollars a week.

Jakob   What's fourteen dollars a week?

David   It's what I needed to bring in, to save, what our business should have brought me in, and then some.

Jakob   And that gets you what, Doovey?

David   A little place, a place I saw in Long Island, just a little place, a suburban life.

Jakob   Is that what you want?

David   Fourteen dollars a week paid out over say nine years is a place, is something owned, possessed . . . is a man's promise to his wife kept, that's fourteen dollars a week over nine years.

Jakob   Owned? What the hell is owned?

David   And how long is it since the end of the war, Jakob? (*Beat.*) Five years. Five years already with a promise not kept . . . I know the business is nothing to you, a sideline, but people are getting prosperous now. You know I'm the only guy I know in business who most weeks last year never brought home no salary.

Jakob   This is Rachel talking, talking through you.

David   Dammit, it's a man's promise kept.

Rachel *enters from the kitchen, visibly pregnant, wrapped in a heavy trailing sweater of* **David**'*s over her home-made party dress. The men stand.*

Jakob   Hello, Rachel.

Rachel   Hello, Jakob.

Jakob   We came a little early to see if we could help out before people got here.

Rachel   That's nice. Only a couple of people, though.

She kisses him perfunctorily.

Jakob   How you feeling, Miss May Day?

Rachel   I've not felt like Miss May Day for a little while now, Jakob.

Jakob   We've not seen enough of you lately, Rachel. Either of you.

Rachel   You know how relations grow away. Connected but apart. Like the roots of a tree.

Jakob   Now has Matthew said hello to his aunt?

Rachel *(softens, smiles)*   No.

Jakob   Who's a rude little man, then?

*He picks **Matthew** up from the pram. He hands the little bundle of baby to **Rachel**. At this moment **Esther** re-enters from the kitchen, wearing a tatty apron. They all watch **Rachel** with the baby. She talks to **Matthew**.*

Rachel   You handsome little boy, aren't you, and so quiet, such a good boy –

Esther   Jake's stupidly proud of him.

David   I bet he is.

Esther   I get up in the night for a glass of water and I find Jake sitting at the table talking to the baby's cot. Telling him about . . . what do you two talk about?

Jakob *(shrugs, thinks, smiles)*   What the world's going to be like when he's grown up. The sort of world it can be. I tell him about my father, what kind of man my father was –

Esther   A sad thing they never met . . .

Jakob   – but oftentimes baseball. Matthew's a committed baseball baby.

*When they look back at **Rachel** they see she has stopped talking to the baby. There are tears in her eyes.*

David   Oh darling no, it's OK.

Esther   Rachel, I'm sorry –

Rachel   It's all right. It's all right . . . Just that, before, I know how much David hoped for a son. He always said otherwise but I knew how much he hoped.

David   No. There's gonna be another baby.

Rachel *hands* **Matthew** *back to* **Jakob**.

Rachel (*collecting herself*)   I'm gonna finish up in the kitchen.

Esther   I'll be in to help you.

Rachel *leaves for the kitchen.* **Esther** *pauses, moves quickly towards* **David**, *kisses him.*

Esther   Listen to Jakob, Doovey.

David   What do you mean?

Esther   Darling Doovey, please listen to him.

She kisses him. **Esther** *leaves.*

David   What does she mean?

Jakob   It'll be all right, Doovey. I promise you that.

David   No Jakob, you can't ever promise me that.

Jakob   You move on.

Beat.

David   What I think is, the baby . . . that it was my fault.

Jakob   How can it be your fault?

David   I brought something into our home. I brought a sickness into our home.

Jakob   What do you mean?

David   You know at Los Alamos . . . well . . . you know that at the centre of the bomb there was a special material. The bomb had a special material, a special sickness.

Jakob   The uranium, you mean? The core?

David   Yeah. But they made a lot of those things at Los Alamos, not just the ones that went for tests or for the Japan bombs. These little hollowed-out sorta hemispheres of uranium. And people stole them, lots of them. A hundred or so went missing. (*Laughs.*) Unbelievable, isn't it? True, though. We took 'em, loads of people, we just took one. People kept them as souvenirs. I took two. One of them, well, you know, but I took two. We kept them, and this is the particularly strange thing about it, we found a use, because they were excellent ashtrays.

Jakob   You're kidding.

David   No. It was in our apartment, this sickness. And then later I started to read in the papers about the stuff that was happening over in Japan. The women who had been made sterile, the women of Hiroshima and Nagasaki. Years after the bombings, the survivors are still dying. So I took this little thing, this evil thing, and wrapped it up and threw it in the sea. But just right after that we lost the baby.

Jakob   No, David, no, it can't be that.

David   But you know what I think sometimes? Sometimes I think it's more than that. Deeper than that. If you do something wrong it will come back. Come back and blight you, like an insect, lay waste to your crops. You understand me, Jake?

Jakob   What did we do wrong?

David   You know.

Jakob   Building the bomb? Our country?

David   You know what we did, Jakob.

Silence.

Jakob   We need to talk, David. We need to talk before the people get here.

David   What's there to talk about, Jakob?

Jakob   A man called Elliot Harvey.

David   I don't know that name.

Jakob   No. And he doesn't know your name. But he knows your face, who you were.

David (*uneasy*)   Who is he?

Jakob   A friend of my friend. A friend who came to you once, you and Rachel, when you were in the desert.

David   I don't want to talk about that now.

Jakob   We need to talk now, David.

David   What, about the man in the desert?

Jakob   They have him. The FBI have him. They have Elliot Harvey.

They're aware of the women in the other room.

David   That plump guy? That matters? But it was so long ago. The war was long ago.

Jakob   The war's not finished, David. The sides, they just got a little shifted around, that's all.

David   Well, what you want me to do about it?

Jakob   They have him, David, and they will get to him, break him. He's just a weak man, just a man that wanted a little bit of money. They break weak men, David.

David   It's so long ago.

Jakob   Not to them. Not at all.

David   Jakob, what do you want me to do?

Jakob   We are not safe, David. We are not safe. Our family is not safe.

Pause.

Tomorrow I'm gonna meet another friend of mine. He has ten thousand dollars for you. I want you to go to Mexico, and from there to Europe. There will be arrangements for you to go to Czechoslovakia, and then . . . a little further.

David (*genuinely surprised*)   You want me to leave? Leave my home? And what about Rachel?

Jakob   There are papers for Rachel.

David   For Rachel too? She's not strong enough to travel. (*Pause.*) But when would we come back?

Pause. He understands.

Not to come back? But how could I leave here? How could I leave my country?

Jakob   What's a country? A country's nothing, don't you know that yet? They have Elliot Harvey, David, they have the man in the desert.

David   What do you expect me to do? Jakob, this isn't what I wanted, what we wanted.

Jakob   Keep your voice down. You have to go, David, you have to go soon.

David   And to go there? To go east? You know what they're saying, Jake – the killings, what they do to people there?

Jakob   It's lies. Never happened.

David (*standing, with great and controlled anger*)   This is easy for you, isn't it, Jakob? What kinda man are you? You don't even feel it. This is where I'm from. For you to send me away and not to feel it even? Send my family away? I could knock you down, Jake, I could –

Suddenly, from the kitchen, the sound of screaming: fear and shock all at once.

Esther (*off*)   David! Jakob! Fire! She's burning! David!

Jakob *and* **David** *run into the kitchen. For a moment the front room is empty.* **Matthew** *starts to cry, quietly at first, but getting louder.*

David *re-enters carrying his wife, the burning clothes literally ripped from her back. His hands are burnt raw. She is screaming in agony. He lays her gently on the sofa.* **Jakob** *and* **Esther** *come in behind them. Everyone is speaking quickly, almost on top of each other.*

David   What happened? Oh Jesus God, what happened –

Rachel   – my baby my baby, oh Doovey it hurts me –

Esther *(out of breath)*   It was the gas heater. The portable. The sweater she had on –

Rachel   – my baby, keep my baby, it hurts me, burning me right along my nerves –

Esther   – the sweater, it caught the flame and she just went up, just burning –

Jakob *has gone to the phone.*

Jakob *(into the phone)*   Ambulance. I need an ambulance. Lafayette Street. 155 Lafayette Street. What? A woman, a woman burning alive –

The baby is crying harder as **Rachel** *screams.* **David** *tries to touch her but she moves away.*

David   Oh Jesus God, what do I do, tell me what I should do.

This scene ends. Different light.

Rachel, *healed, stands from the sofa, picks up a long jacket and puts it on. She walks a long, looping cross right around the limits of the stage, through time. She walks, eventually, into* **Anna**'s *apartment in 1975.* **Anna** *is sitting, reading from the Rubenstein transcripts. She looks up, sees* **Rachel**.

Anna   Hi, Mum. I was expecting you.

Fast blackout.

Interval.

Act Three

Scene One

1975.

New York.

Anna Girshfeld's *apartment, a moment later.* **Anna** *sits in her chair.* **Rachel** *is vulnerable with her daughter, fragile.*

Rachel You were expecting me?

Anna Yeah.

She puts the trial transcript down on a pile of school books she has been marking.

Rachel What I mean is, I know. I know you were expecting me. The letter you sent me. Like a subpoena.

Anna I didn't order you to come here.

Rachel But you knew I would.

Anna Yeah.

Silence.

You gonna sit down or what, Mom? Because the thing is that I have someone coming. Pretty soon.

Rachel You want for me to go?

Anna (*shrugs*) And to come back.

Rachel You want me to come back?

Anna Yes.

Rachel Come back when? Come back later tonight?

Anna (*smiles*) Maybe that's not such a good idea. I may be a little busy later.

Rachel You're going out?

She finally sits on the corner of a chair.

Anna   Oh no, staying in.

Rachel   Who do you have coming here? A man?

Anna   Yeah, a man.

Rachel   And you're going to ask him to spend the night?

Anna   I think maybe I already asked him. If not he may just ask himself.

Rachel   Anna. Who is this man?

Anna   Shocked, Mom?

Rachel   Shocked, no.

Anna   Not very radical for a once famous radical.

Rachel   Well, that was different.

Anna   Less sex, more violence.

Rachel   Anna –

Anna   You know, everybody I know my age says how striking it is that our generation is so much more radical than their parents'. Well, we're not quite like that in my family, I say. Then I stop talking, 'cause of course we don't talk about my family in my family.

Rachel   That's enough, Anna.

Anna   So, sit down, Mum.

Rachel   OK.

She sits. Pause.

Anna   You know what a scapegoat is, Mom? Something that needs to be consumed. The part of you that's guilty, part of you that you don't like, you put it outside you and you destroy it. One of my kids just wrote me about it. Real smart kid, she loves all the Greek myths.

Pause.

Rachel   What you said in your letter, it hurt me. Hurt your father.

Anna   What I said in my letter?

Rachel   Yes. Your father doesn't need to see that from his own daughter.

Anna   People'd say he needs to be hurt. People'd say you both need to be hurt.

Rachel   Let me explain to you what happened –

Anna   I think it's time for me to find out what was true about Jakob and Esther –

Rachel   You want to know about Esther? You want to know the truth about Esther? When they read out the verdicts she sang. She sang a song from an opera. Right there in the courtroom. Esther only wanted to be the heroine of her own life, that's what's true –

Anna   I said time for me to find it out, not for you to tell me –

Rachel   But your father, Anna, think of your father –

Anna   You of all people aren't going to tell me families need to stick together. You heard that new joke. A man is having business trouble with his brother-in-law. His wife tells him to remember that she loves him. 'Oh sure,' says the guy. 'I love him too, love him like a brother . . . like David Girshfeld loves brothers.' Something like that, joke goes something like that –

Rachel   This was done for you Anna, for you

Anna   Don't tell me what you've done for me, don't ever tell me that –

There's a knock at the door. Silence.

Mum, you have to go now. Please don't be seen here.

Rachel *considers.*

Rachel   Where can I go?

Anna   Out onto the balcony. You can leave down the fire-stairs.

Rachel   The fire-stairs, Anna –

Anna   Go.

She faces her mother down.

If you're seen here you'll be recognised, and that will change things for me –

Rachel   You've seen in your father's eyes what is true –

Anna   No, I don't know that I've ever seen that.

Pause.

Rachel   What a child never understands is that you can be good and bad all at once, in a single action.

She starts to leave. Suddenly moved, **Anna** *goes towards her, catches her, holds her.*

Anna   Mom! Wait ten minutes for me. I'll send him out for coffee or something. Wait on the first stairs.

Rachel *nods and leaves.*

Anna *pats down her hair, moves to the door, unlocks it.* **Matthew** *enters, full of strange energy. He moves towards her, kisses her hard.*

Matthew   You're beautiful.

Anna   Matthew.

Matthew   You speak French?

Anna   A little. Why?

Matthew   '*La vérité est en marche; rien ne peut plus l'arrêter.*'

Anna   I know enough to guess that you're not asking because you're taking me to Paris for a surprise.

Matthew   Not Paris. Something someone taught me when I was a kid. Zola on the Dreyfuss case. 'Truth is on the march, nothing can stop it now.' Nothing.

Beat.

Anna   I've never seen you like this. Like you're high.

Matthew   It's hard to explain, you did it to me, though. There's a fire in me, in my veins, along my nerves. Feel like I've had a moment of recognition, like I've remembered who I am.

Anna   Where have you been the last week?

Matthew   Working. Reading. Working.

Anna   Working on what?

Matthew   I'm going to do it. What you showed me, I'm going to do it.

Anna   Do what?

Matthew   What was left me. The Rubenstein case.

Anna   You're going to help with the committee?

Matthew   Yeah, I'm going to help with the committee. No, I'm going to do more than help . . . I don't know how to start this conversation. I need to ask you something.

Anna   OK.

Pause. **Matthew** *can't find the words.*

Anna   You know you haven't said anything out loud yet?

Matthew   Yeah.

Anna   So?

Matthew   Can I be sure of you?

Anna   What do you mean?

Matthew   I mean you know how we're scared all the time, however old we are, scared of what people see in us, of things we've done and not done. Scared to be known. And we're real good at covering this, with a toughness that's all cracked and gaping at the edges. But what we really want is someone, like when we were kids, somebody we can just be sure of. That's what I'm asking.

Pause.

Anna   I remember one night when I was a kid I'd done something wrong. I don't remember what it was, but I remember that I was kind of sick with that afraid feeling you have when you're a kid and you've done something wrong and you just know you're going to get found out. I was just a little girl. Things were pretty tough for my parents when I was a little girl. My father was away, and so I went to my mother. And I told my mother what I had done and I remember how she looked at me, like she was sad and happy altogether, and she said whatever I ever did wrong it wouldn't matter to her, even if it was the worst thing in the world, and she told me to remember this always because this was what love was. Whatever I did it wouldn't matter.

Matthew   So?

Anna   So you can be sure of me, Matthew Maddison. I love you.

Matthew   I love you.

Pause

I'll show you what I wanted to say. Where's your phone? I need your phone.

Anna   Here.

Matthew *stands, walks to the phone, pulls a piece of notepaper from his pocket. As he dials, his eyes stay on* **Anna**.

Matthew   So there's this guy Bayliss running the Rubenstein committee.

Anna   Yeah, sure.

Matthew   Yeah, hello, can I get Tom Bayliss? Thank you. OK. I'll wait. Hi, is that Mr Bayliss? Oh OK, he's not there. (*To* **Anna**, *his hand over the receiver.*) Not there. I guess I didn't inherit the family talent for dramatic gesture – (*Into the phone.*) No, I'm not from a newspaper. No, no, I'm not from the FBI. Yeah, I'll leave a message. My number is . . . No wait, just say I'll call back. My name? (*After a small hesitation.*) My name is Matthew Rubenstein. Tell him that Matthew Rubenstein wants to speak to him . . . Yeah, I guess you know how to spell the name . . . Yeah, that's right, I am who you think I am. Yeah, I'm here on Anna Levi's number this afternoon. (*He replaces the receiver.*) I am who you think I am.

Pause.

Anna   The son.

Matthew   The son.

Pause. **Anna** *sits.*

Anna   What are the chances?

Matthew   Considering where we met? Certainly above average.

Anna   Yeah.

Pause.

Matthew   It's that I want to speak now. It's time to speak now.

Anna   What will you say?

Matthew   My name is a good start. And what is true. Guess I'll have to talk about that for a while. After that we'll see what we see.

Anna   How did you know to tell me now?

Matthew   What do you mean?

Anna   I mean, why now? Because of the documents, because – ?

Matthew   When I was with you it made me remember who I am. You let me remember my anger, and how much of it was good and true. I am twenty-six years old and you made me realise that it was time to become myself again. And I feel cloaked in it, cloaked in purpose, and it's the purest feeling I can remember in my whole life –

Anna   Matthew –

Matthew   – and I have read these transcripts and these
documents and called people who haven't seen me since
I was four years old and I have found that there is a case
to be made and a case to be answered, a case that can be
made against the murderers, against the cannibals that ate
my family alive. And because of who I am if I make the
case people will listen. And it feels like a holy duty, it feels
sacred, and I knew all my life that this thing was mine to do.

And you know the strange thing? With this in front of me,
this thing to do, I feel kinda happier than I've ever felt
before. You see, you can't deny yourself, you can't deny the
memory that history holds within your body, the life lived
even before you lived, the life before you were born. It sort
of takes away the sense of you as you and just shows you
what you have to do. And I realise today that I've been
waiting for this feeling, this pure feeling, all my adult life,
and I got it from you. Never realised it would come from
another person, always thought it was me, just me.

Pause. **Anna** *is crying without concealment.*

Anna   Matthew, what is it you think you want? What is it
you think will happen?

Matthew   I want my lost ones back. I want them back,
want them back true, like they were.

Anna   Matthew, it won't be like you think it will –

Matthew   The day they burnt my parents alive I played
baseball in the yard with a social worker. I can still feel the
ball in my hand, too big for my child's hand, how it felt that
day when they told me that my parents had been burnt
alive. But my hand is a man's hand now. And now I know
what to do.

The phone rings. They don't move. After several rings **Anna** *picks it up.*

Anna   Hello. You're calling for who? Oh, I understand.
Yeah, he's here. Oh, how did I find him? He found me. (*To*

Matthew.) It's Tom Bayliss calling for Matthew Rubenstein, calling for you.

Matthew *takes the phone.*

Matthew   This is Matthew . . . Thank you for calling back . . . Well I guess it's time to claim my inheritance, you know. Yeah, that's fine. I can meet this afternoon . . . I have your address . . . OK, good.

He puts the phone down. Silence. They stand at opposite sides of the room.

Tell me what you think of me.

Anna   I wish you were how I wished you were.

Matthew   I didn't lie. I didn't lie. My name is Maddison. It was changed after I was adopted.

Anna   A sin of omission.

Matthew   No sin.

He moves towards her. She shifts away from him.

You can't bear to touch me, can you?

*After a moment, **Anna** walks to him, stops two feet away. Bending her hand back she runs the inside of her wrist along the line of his cheek, down to his chin and then away.*

Anna   Let me call you.

Matthew   What is that?

Anna   I'll call you.

Matthew   'Let me call you,' what is that?

Anna   You have this thing to do now, Matthew.

Matthew   But what you said, before –

Anna   I know what I said.

*Finally **Matthew** nods, moves towards the door.*

Anna   Matthew, wait. Why were you there in the first place?

Matthew   In the first place?

Anna   The gallery, why were you there?

Matthew   I – I don't have a copy of that picture. I don't have any of the famous ones.

Anna   You could have got one. You could have got a print. For you to sit there, though –

Matthew   It's the people's faces. That's why I went there. The people's faces when they see the picture. Really. The kindness in people's faces when they see it, their empathy. It's a talent, empathy, a gift, that's what no one understands. Seeing the truth in other people's lives. The picture gives them that. I like to see it on them, the bloom of that talent.

She nods. He waits and then leaves. As his footsteps disappear, she moves to the door, locks it, puts on the chain. She starts to cry, deep, gulping for air. After a moment, **Rachel** *enters from the fire-stairs. She moves cautiously towards* **Anna**, *wants to take her in her arms.*

Rachel   It will be all right, Anna, it will be all right.

Anna *faces her mother down, will not let her close the distance between them.*

Anna   It won't ever be all right. That's what I just heard. Don't you see it? Whatever I do, it won't be all right, it will never be all right.

Rachel *stands by the door, unsure whether to leave. Finally she goes.*

Scene Two

The action in the secene is split between the two periods: June 1951 – an FBI interview room, US District Courthouse, New York; and 1975 – the kitchen of **David** *and* **Rachel**'s *house, suburbs of New York.*

Lights up on the interview room. **Jakob** *sits at the table in his shirtsleeves. After a moment,* **Paul Cranmer**, *an FBI agent, enters.* **Cranmer** *is a gentle, clever man, wearing a suit he is proud of and carrying a bundle of papers. He sits opposite* **Jakob**.

Cranmer   I'm Paul Cranmer.

Jakob   Jakob Rubenstein.

Cranmer   I just read this a couple of hours ago to your brother. It helped him, I think.

Jakob   OK.

Cranmer   Someone gave it to me when I was coming in here today. Off the radio. A sort of recipe.

Jakob   You going to read it or tell me?

Cranmer   In order to provide the best care to severe burns victims you require forty-two tanks of oxygen, 2.7 miles of gauze and forty pints of correct type blood for transfusion purposes. Do you think that's forty-two tanks of oxygen a day or for the entire treatment period?

Jakob   I don't know.

Cranmer   Your brother might have known that. What with your sister being burnt so recently. He told me that he even had to go on the radio to appeal for blood, because your sister has a rare type and she was sick. But to find forty pints, though, that's kind of a problem, right?

Jakob   Not my sister.

Cranmer   Excuse me?

Jakob   My wife's brother. My brother-in-law. His wife. Not my sister.

Cranmer   His wife Rachel?

Jakob   Yes.

Cranmer   It's just that I was told that you're a close family.

Jakob   David told you that?

Cranmer   Yes.

Jakob   We are.

Cranmer   Your sister, her baby, it lived, right?

Jakob   It lived.

Cranmer   Boy or girl?

Jakob   Girl. Anna.

Cranmer   The other part of the recipe is sort of a question. Planners have calculated that in the event of an atomic attack on New York among the casualties there will be a hundred thousand people suffering from severe burns. Where do you think the city might find four million pints of blood, some of it rare?

Lights down on the interview room. Lights up on the kitchen, 1975. It's five a.m. **Anna** *enters, switches on a lamp on the table. She sits, listens for noise in the house. She opens her purse, takes out a bottle of pills. She counts ten into her hand, lines them out on the table. She moves to the sink, pours a glass of water, returns to her chair. She considers the pills. Then, one by one, she starts to take them. Lights down on kitchen.*

Lights up on the interview room.

Cranmer   David told me that you are in business together?

Jakob   That's right. Making parts.

Cranmer   And what does David do?

Jakob   He's a machinist. He can make things.

Cranmer   Good at it?

Jakob   Yeah.

Cranmer   Where'd he learn that?

Jakob   In the war.

Cranmer   Where'd he fight?

Jakob   He didn't fight. He made stuff. He was out in the desert someplace, I think.

Cranmer   The desert. Where'd you fight, Jakob?

Jakob   I was exempt. Because of my work. I was in the Signals Corps.

Cranmer   In uniform?

Jakob   No, a civilian.

Cranmer   I was in the 101st Normandy, Bastogne, into Germany even.

Jakob   I'd have fought them too. It was just my health was not so strong and I had abilities.

Cranmer (*with a nod*)   You'd have fought them?

Jakob   The Fascists.

Cranmer   I was fighting the enemies of my country.

Jakob   That's what I meant.

Cranmer   David says the business isn't going too good.

Jakob   It's been a little difficult lately.

Cranmer   Told me that he'd borrowed money off you.

Jakob   Yes.

Cranmer   How much?

Jakob   A little here and there.

Cranmer   He says about a thousand dollars in total. In payments of maybe two hundred dollars a time.

Jakob   Maybe. I don't know.

Cranmer   That was big of you, Jakob.

Jakob   We're a close family.

Cranmer   It's just with the business not going so well, where'd you get the money?

Jakob   We save a little better than David and Rachel. I'm a little older.

Cranmer   You serve out the war, Jakob?

Jakob   What do you mean?

Cranmer   I mean were you still working for the Signals department at the end of the war?

Jakob   I left a little before.

Cranmer   Left?

Jakob   Yeah.

Cranmer   It says here that you were dismissed because you gave false information relating to your earlier membership of the Communist Party of the United States.

Pause.

Elliot Harvey, a courier for the Soviets, has identified David Girshfeld as a contact.

Pause.

It's time to speak now Jakob.

Jakob   Speak?

Cranmer   David Girshfeld has told us that whilst working on the Manhattan Project to build the atomic bomb at Los Alamos, New Mexico, he stole descriptions of the bomb, samples of uranium and made sketches illustrating the practical physics behind the construction of an implosion bomb in order to give this information to the government of the Soviet Union. He told us that he gave this information to a Soviet courier. He told us that this operation was set up and orchestrated by his brother Jakob Rubenstein, the leader of a Soviet spy network here in the United States.

Jakob (*shocked*)   Doovey said that?

Cranmer   It's time to speak now, Jakob. We both know enough to know how this ends. It's not the movies. Every Red spy we've caught has squealed. A professional arrangement. You speak, we make a deal and we move on.

Jakob   But David said that?

Cranmer   Yeah, that's what he said. So you need to tell me your involvement. You need to give me the names of your contacts, both Russian and American, and sign your name to it and then we'll deal.

Pause. **Jakob** *makes a first decision.*

Jakob   He's lying.

Cranmer   Jakob. We have you. Name the names and we move on.

Jakob   He's lying. David Girshfeld is lying. I will not sign my father's name to David Girshfeld.

Pause.

I . . . earlier I said something which wasn't true.

Cranmer   OK.

Jakob   We are a close family but there have been . . . problems in the business. They've been ripping us up lately. David particularly. He's been angry with me 'cause I had to put people above him, even though he's partner. People to supervise. He wanted to think of himself as one of the big guys, you know, a boss.

Cranmer (*not convinced*)   You saying he made this up because of a personal argument?

Jakob   Well, David – ·he was real angry about this, you know, kinda simmering with it. And then when Rachel got hurt – it unbalances a man, to see his wife in pain.

Cranmer   Yeah, it does. Do you know the name Elliot Harvey, Jakob? Or Valentin Geller, a KGB agent in the United States. Or maybe Geller's American lover, Sarah Stampe?

Jakob   I don't know those names.

Cranmer   Tell me the truth and this ends good and we move on.

Jakob   This is the truth.

Cranmer   When Sarah Stampe confessed she told us that Geller regularly met with a man, a New York man, a New

York Jew. She gave us something she'd overheard in a telephone conversation, what we thought was a code-name. You know what it was?

Jakob *doesn't respond.*

Cranmer   God, we thought we were being so smart with that. We had top guys working on that. You know what the unbreakable code-word she overheard was? It was 'Jakob'.

Pause.

Jakob   You gotta ask yourself what kinda man would put his brother in this sort of place. Put his own family in this place.

Cranmer   Maybe there's something bigger than family to him. Maybe that's why you're sitting here too, telling me this fiction. Because you think there's something bigger.

Jakob   I mean, what is that? A man who will tell lies against his blood, his flesh, just because he got himself in trouble. That's a man lower than dogs, a man worse than a criminal.

Cranmer   Worse than a man who would give the bomb to the enemy of his country?

Jakob   Yeah, but Mr Cranmer when he says he did those things, that country, the Soviet Union, it wasn't an enemy of ours. They fought the Fascists too, they fought with us.

Cranmer   Is that how you see what he did?

Jakob   No, not precisely, but a man could see it like that, I guess.

Cranmer   You know how many American boys are dying in Korea each day to fight those people who used to be our allies?

Jakob   Yeah –

Cranmer   These bombs they were made to be used against countries –

Jakob   Yeah, I understand that, Mr Cranmer –

Cranmer   David says you were the one who told him how valuable this information could be to the Reds. He says your wives were there when you did it.

Jakob   But Mr Cranmer, can you ascertain a man like that, can you ascertain a man that would lie about his own sister and her husband?

Cranmer   David Girshfeld says you were responsible for giving the atomic bomb to the Russians –

Jakob   He's a liar –

Cranmer   You want to kill yourself, Jakob, you a jumper, is that it – ?

Jakob   You bring him here, Mr Cranmer. Is he here? You bring him here and I'll call him a liar to his face –

Lights down on the interview room. Lights up on the kitchen.

Anna *sits, her eyes closed.* **David** *enters, cautiously. He wears a dressing gown. He is fifty-three years old.*

David   Is anyone in here? I heard a noise, is anyone in here?

Pause.

I'll call the FBI, you realise? I have the number ready by the phone. Right by the phone.

He moves heavily towards the phone.

Anna   It's me.

David   Anna?

Anna   Yeah, it's Anna . . . A little jumpy, Dad?

David   I heard noises.

Anna   Did I wake you?

David   No. I was awake already.

Anna   Still not sleeping through the night?

David   There's been this new interest lately. I get a little worried for intrusions.

Anna   I know.

David *walks to the refrigerator.*

David   You want a glass of milk?

Anna   No.

David *pours himself a big glass of milk.*

David   You remember when you were a little girl and you'd come down for milk in the early morning 'cause you knew that I'd be awake then? And we'd have the milk and then get cleaned up and your mother would never realise how I got you ready for school so quick. And it was 'cause we started the whole thing off at five in the morning. I liked that. I liked that we kept it secret.

Anna   You like to keep secrets, Dad?

David *sits.*

David   What do you mean?

Anna   Mom came to see me.

David   I know.

Anna   Because of the letter. Because of what I've been doing.

David   It's taken care of.

Anna   What do you mean?

David   I called a guy.

Anna   Who?

David   A guy from before. He'll take care of it.

Anna   I knew that if I came at this time you'd be sitting upstairs 'cause you couldn't sleep through the night. Sitting reading maybe, or having an early morning bath, and that you'd hear the noise and come down and you'd be the one to find me.

David   Yeah, well, I still hear the noises in the night.

Anna   Did I hurt you?

David   You know I read in a newspaper yesterday that some word-smart guy said there were no second acts in American lives. Well, I can tell that guy that's bullshit. I've been living it twenty years and more. An unremarked second act, until now.

Anna   I think it was a writer. Fitzgerald maybe.

David   But I wanted to be like that, unremarked. Walled off from the world – there's an old word for that, read it once, when they bricked the people up in their rooms, an oubl – (*He can't pronounce the word.*)

Anna   An oubliette, Dad. It's a French word.

David   Yeah, but I wanted to be safe like that.

Anna   It was a torture, Dad. A means of torture.

David   Sounds like safety to me.

Anna   You don't want history to remember you good?

David   Don't care. Don't care. Ain't going to be around when that happens.

Anna   But you're a famous man.

David   No, not a famous man, never wanted to be that. Jakob was a famous man. Wanted to be a famous man. Most famous suicide in American history.

Anna   What did you want to be?

David   I just wanted to make things. I liked the tampering with stuff. The finding which wire went into which socket. I liked having stuff, real stuff, in my hands, feeling it change. I liked coming to the sink with dirty hands after a day, scrubbing them clean, washing the day off them and sitting down to eat a meal. Jakob wanted something else. Afterwards I always thought Jake would have got on better with the guys in the desert. Those men, the scientists, they worked with things which weren't real, tried to twist them till they were, lived in their heads. Jakob was like that. It was only in prison that I really started to read at all, learn words better.

Anna   What I've been doing, really it was because there was a question I've wanted to ask you since I was a little girl.

David   Yeah?

Anna   Never had the guts to ask it, though.

David   What question?

Anna   How you did what you did. To Jakob, to your sister. How you gave them away.

Pause.

David   What'd you want me to have done? When the FBI came after me, what the hell, you want me to pull out a gun and start shooting? I mean I wasn't a criminal, I wasn't in the mob. Apart from the crime of the century, I never even got a traffic citation.

Anna   I don't mean that. I mean after.

David   I didn't live with my sister, my sister didn't have my children. You make a life with someone. A commitment of life. That's more important than a sister. For people my age, that's more important.

Anna   You thought Mom was threatened?

David (*his emotions have been rising*)   It was a battle to the death. Sometimes family is a battle to the death –

Anna   And you chose your sister's death –

David   No, I did not choose that. They chose that. They chose that, for themselves. Any time they could have cleared themselves. They died 'cause of that and it was the most stupid, sick thing any person could choose. They died for something that don't exist, they died for their own lies.

Anna   And you were smart and saved yourself.

David   I won't ask no one for forgiveness for that. Your mother never put one foot in a jail except to visit me. A man stands up, Anna, a man stands up.

Anna   Dad, when was the last time you slept through the night?

David   The night of my arrest. I'd had a long day before they came for me. And later I was tired after all the talking. So it was a relief to be in a bed, any bed. And I slept through the night. When I woke up I was surprised how deep that sleep was. Thought maybe they'd given me something, you know, like a serum.

Anna   That was twenty-five years ago.

David   Twenty-four. June 17th 1951.

Anna   You remember the date?

David   Special day.

Anna   How can you sit and lie to me now? How can you lie to me now? You don't sleep through the night because you're afraid. You live in your head, don't think I don't know that. You don't sleep through the night because you still don't know whether what you did was right.

David   There was a word that I didn't fully understand.

Anna   What do you mean?

Pause

David   They were working on me, trying to play me. The agents. But I didn't understand what they were looking for until later. But they wanted a lever, a way to put pressure on Jakob. They said was your sister Esther 'cognisant' of Jakob's activities?

Anna   You mean did she know what was going on?

David   Yeah. But I thought . . . I thought it meant something else. At first that's what I thought.

Anna   And you said she was?

David   Yeah. I mean, however little she did, she still knew. But that's not why I said yes. But that was a moment, a first moment. I think about that sometimes. Jake wouldn't have made that mistake. But Jake would never have squealed. He wanted to be a saint, a martyr, wanted to be dead. Those are the words people use about Jake. There were different words for me, later. A Judas, a rat. That's what they say about me. But I can say to you that on that day I stood up. But still I think sometimes I made a mistake in that first moment, made a mistake with the words.

Anna (*simply, surprised and suddenly touched*)   You made a mistake with the words.

David   Yeah, I did.

Anna   Dad.

David   I thought that it meant . . . it doesn't matter, but I thought it was something different . . . I was just a guy, you know, just a guy.

Anna *looks into her father, sees him. This is the closest point of contact in their lives.*

Anna   Sometimes I wish I'd known you, Dad.

David   I would've liked that.

Pause.

But I tell you something.

Anna   What?

David   Trying to say what could have happened if something else had happened different, it's impossible, like trying to tell the future.

Lights down on the kitchen. Lights up on the interview room. **David** *walks through time into 1951.* **Jakob** *sits at the interview table.*

Cranmer *stands between the two men, a little back.* **David** *is nervous, exhausted. There is fury in the room.*

Jakob   David, what are you doing?

David   Jakob, you know exactly what I'm doing.

Jakob   Whatever you've done wrong up to this point, David, I don't know, I don't know what it is. But today, what you do today, what're you're doing now, this is the moment when you decide what kind of man you are.

Pause.

David   A man came to me in the desert. A short man, a kinda plump man. And he waited in the hall whilst I drew diagrams from memory which described how to make an atomic weapon –

Jakob   Jesus, David, don't you understand what's happening here? A man stands up, when he's in trouble, on his own he stands up –

David   Tell them, Jakob. Tell them and we can go home. Tell them and clear yourself –

Jakob   Clear myself? You don't understand what you're saying. To give them this, to confess when I haven't done the thing they want me to confess to, that means I can't ever be clear –

Cranmer   What he means is this: save yourself –

Jakob   How can I be saved if I give myself up to this, to these lies – ?

David   They'll kill us, Jakob. Haven't they told you what they'll do? They'll strap us into a chair and to kill us they will burn our brains –

Cranmer   Tell me your contacts. Tell me who is in your network.

Jakob   I will not give myself up to this –

David   This fight we can't win, Jake –

Jakob (*with great feeling*)   Every day you fight, you understand me, you fight always and every day, even those battles you can't win, and then and only then the world changes.

Pause. **Jakob** *is distant now.*

David   Jake, please, do this thing.

Jakob *doesn't respond.*

David   Jakob, do you know what day it is?

Jakob   Sunday, David. It's Sunday. Sunday the what, the sixteenth?

Cranmer   The seventeenth.

Jakob   What does it matter?

David   It's Father's Day, Jakob. I have to go home and give the baby her formula.

Jakob   Nobody going home tonight, David, don't you understand that yet?

David   Mr Cranmer, my wife is in the hospital, so I have to go home and give the baby her formula. I could promise to come back here after. Or you could send someone with me –

Cranmer   The Bureau will have someone looking after your baby.

Silence. **David** *is close to tears.*

Cranmer   David, what we spoke about earlier, tell me again. Where you were when Jakob first suggested that you could obtain information about the bomb.

David   We were in their apartment in Knickerbocker Village.

Cranmer   We?

David   Jakob and I and Esther.

Cranmer   And so Esther wasn't just aware of it, she was involved?

Jakob   David −

David   She was just sitting at the table, making some food, she wasn't doing much −

Cranmer   But she was involved with the discussions −

David   Well, she was there −

Cranmer   − she was in the room, she knew about it, spoke about it −

David   I said she was there −

Cranmer   − so Esther *was* involved with the plot to steal the bomb − ?

David   Yeah, dammit, maybe she was −

Something happens in the room, a motion of violence.

Jakob   Don't you see it? They're trying to kill my wife. (*He stands, taking deep breaths.*) How can you call yourself a man? How can you call yourself a man when you give them this? Don't you see what they're doing?

Cranmer   Sit down, Jakob. David, get out. (*Shouting to outside the door.*) Get him out of here! Sit down, Jakob.

David *leaves the room.*

Cranmer   Be smart now, Jakob.

Jakob *doesn't reply. After a moment* **Cranmer** *moves to go. As he reaches the door, he pauses.*

Cranmer   What you said, somebody else said that to me once before.

Jakob   What I said?

Cranmer   That you fight every day, even the battles that you can't win.

Jakob   Who?

Cranmer   My lieutenant. In the war. At Bastogne, Battle of the Bulge, January '45. The Nazis had counter-attacked.

We were surrounded, dug in deep, in a forest in midwinter, running low on ammunition, the shells falling. He was just a kid. But he said what you said. He was a good man.

Jakob   What people don't understand is that the war's inside us as well as outside. Fought inside, against our nerves, the sinews of our thought. Understand that. If you burn me from the inside out, that's why you'll be doing it.

Cranmer   We won that battle, lot of kids didn't come back, but we won it.

Jakob   You got kids of your own?

Cranmer   No.

Jakob   They're born in blood and screams. New stuff is born in blood and horror.

Cranmer   I saw that in Bastogne.

He leaves.

Lights down on the interview room. Lights up on the kitchen. **David** *has walked back to 1975.*

David   Heh, you want to know about fame? The day I was released from prison, the last day of my being a famous man, I didn't even make the front page. You know why? Clark Gable died, aged fifty-nine years. He'd been making a movie out in the desert, I think. Clark Gable, there was a hell of an actor. You know that was the same day?

Anna   Yeah, Dad, I knew that.

David   Clark Gable kept me off the front pages, and I was surprised, that's how famous I was. (*With feeling.*) You talk about history. All I want is to be forgotten.

Anna   Dad, you know the mornings when we'd drink the milk together before the sun came properly up? You know why it was some mornings and not others that I came down to you? It was the mornings you took those early baths. I woke up to the sound of the water moving through the pipes, mechanical and natural all at once. I always thought how cold the water must have been for you.

David   I never figured that. (*Smiles.*) They were cold, those baths. But I liked the privacy of them, the privacy of the early morning. (*He stands.*) I'm gonna go put some clothes on. You'll stay for breakfast, Anna? Just you and me?

She nods. He moves towards the stairs and stops.

I remember the sound of water through the pipes, though. But not from here. From prison, the nights in prison.

He leaves. **Anna** *moves quickly to the sink, puts fingers down her throat. She vomits. She repeats the process, again and again, trying to purge her system of the remains of the pills. She sinks to her knees, shaking.*

Act Four

Scene One

June 1953.

The Death House, Sing Sing Prison.

An interview room. **Esther** *sits at a table. She is thirty-eight years old. She is singing quietly to herself: 'Un Bel Dì' from* Madame Butterfly. **Cranmer** *enters, tense, on edge. He is carrying a new briefcase.* **Esther** *continues to sing, gently.*

Cranmer   Hello, Esther.

Esther   I don't know who you are.

Cranmer   I'm Paul Cranmer.

Esther *(shrugs)*   Don't know who you are.

Cranmer   FBI. I arrested your husband two years ago.

Esther   OK.

Pause.

Cranmer *(gesturing to the briefcase, from which he takes papers)* Someone just bought this for me. A gift.

Pause.

What you were singing, what is that? I've heard that before somewhere.

Esther   You like opera, Mr Cranmer?

Cranmer   Some.

Esther   You know opera?

Cranmer   Yeah. And through my wife a little.

Esther   I had recordings of many operas, before. I would save for them. My husband would buy them for me sometimes, as a gift.

Cranmer   That's nice.

Esther   It's Puccini. 'Un Bel Di'. 'One Fine Day'. From *Madame Butterfly*.

Pause.

Cranmer   Ten days to go.

Esther   Ten days, Mr Cranmer.

Pause.

Cranmer   I'm here to help you, Esther. Help you and Jakob. You need to understand that before we go on.

Esther   OK.

Cranmer   And you need to know that I've been trying to help you for a little while now. That my reputation has been altered by it –

Esther (*smiles*)   Altered?

Cranmer   – kinda tarnished because of it. Hoover calls me Paul the Convert. The road to Damascus, you know, thinks I'm a bleeding heart –

Esther   Dangerous thing to be right now, Mr Cranmer –

Cranmer   I'll survive –

Esther (*mocking*)   Oh Mr Cranmer, that's what we thought, too.

Cranmer   I'm here to help you. To offer you your life. Your lives.

Esther   Go on.

Cranmer   I don't have anything complicated to give. Just your life. Confess. Tell the government what you know. Confess and live.

Pause.

That's the deal. It wasn't meant to be like this. Meant to be like dominoes, falling.

Esther   You know the story of *Madame Butterfly*?

Cranmer   A little.

Esther   Butterfly is a Japanese woman, who marries an American sailor, a wandering man, a man that couldn't be held. After their wedding he leaves Japan. Butterfly has his child, a son. Butterfly's servants think he will never come back to her. But Butterfly is pure in her hope, not tainted. And then one day his ship comes back and he has an American wife with him, made a new alliance. Because a person she loves has betrayed her, she decides the only honourable solution is to die and she kills herself with the sword of her father.

Pause.

Cranmer   What happens to the child?

Esther   What?

Cranmer   Their son, what happens to him? She leaves him?

Esther   No, she wraps him in the American flag and leaves him for his father, for his future –

Cranmer   You see, what I'm saying, Esther, is –

Esther (*moved by her story*)   'Un bel di . . . One fine day we will see smoke on the horizon and then his ship will appear, white in the harbour.' That's what she sings when everyone tells her he will never come back. Her hope is pure when nobody else's hope is worth a damn. You understand me, Mr Cranmer, her hope is pure because her heart is too, and she is a woman of honour, a mother of honour.

Cranmer   Don't wait for the white ship in the harbour, Esther. There's no white ship coming.

Esther   I will not give up my hope to you, Mr Cranmer.

Cranmer   What are you hoping for, Esther?

Esther   The future.

Cranmer   The future.

Pause.

You know I got married last month.

Esther   I didn't know that.

Cranmer   Met her a year ago. She was a friend of my cousin. Saw her with him one day last June, this beautiful woman, standing outside a dress shop thinking whether she wanted to go in or not. It changes you, getting married, makes you think about the future, right?

Esther   It does.

Cranmer   What does Jakob think about marriage?

Esther   We think the same.

Cranmer   What's that?

Esther   That it matters. Love.

Cranmer   Above all things?

Esther   Above most, yeah.

Cranmer   You see, the thing which has been giving people like me in the Bureau most trouble is your marriage.

Esther   You don't need to worry about my marriage, Mr Cranmer.

Cranmer   I guess what troubles us is, it's kinda hard to know exactly what you really knew, what you really did. Before.

Esther   I'm an innocent woman, Mr Cranmer.

Cranmer   What if you are? That's what people in the Bureau are saying, you understand me?

Esther   No, you tell me what you mean.

Cranmer   I mean people think you're the tough one. That's how people like to see a woman in your position. The smart one. And they want to blame you. But maybe you just

knew a little bit about what your husband was doing, maybe
you just typed a couple of letters, took some calls or just
spoke about it, vaguely, at night when the lights were off and
the apartment was quiet.

Esther   I did nothing wrong.

Cranmer   Well, maybe that's it, Esther. Maybe that's it.
Maybe you were never the driving force behind this –

Esther   You people know nothing about us –

Cranmer   If that were it maybe we could save you from
this.

Esther   Betrayal, that's what you mean.

Cranmer   Maybe you could be the one to save Jakob.

Esther   Like dominoes falling, right?

Pause.

Cranmer   It's just, that's the thing that worries people like
me, you see, when we try to comprehend a marriage like
yours.

Pause.

When I met your husband I didn't hate him for what he'd
done to my country. I thought that I would, but I didn't.
(*Beat.*) I want for you to live. I want for you to go back to
your kid.

Esther *is close to breaking down.*

Cranmer   How often you see Jakob, Esther?

Esther   Weekly. Wednesday, wonderful Wednesday.

Cranmer   Where do you meet?

Esther   They have a room they use for our meetings.

Cranmer   But there's an iron grill between you, right?

Esther   Yeah.

Cranmer   Since when have they used this room?

Esther   Since the beginning.

Cranmer   Two years?

Esther   Yeah.

Cranmer   Then I have a present for you.

Cranmer *stands and walks to the door, bangs on it twice. He turns back to* **Esther** *as they wait.*

Cranmer   So you know Butterfly's Japanese?

Esther   Yeah.

Cranmer   You know where's she from?

Esther (*surprised*)   What do you mean?

Cranmer   Where the story happens, you know where that is?

Esther (*uncertain*)   A city by the sea . . . I don't know.

Cranmer   A city by the sea, that's right. You know the name of the city by the sea? The city is Nagasaki. No white ships in that harbour in '45, after the bomb. When I heard you sang that song after the verdict I thought of that. The bomb your husband gave to the Russians. We know everything, Esther. We've known for two years. Confess and live.

Esther *is silent.* **Jakob** *is ushered into the interview room. He is thirty-seven years old.* **Cranmer** *unlocks his cuffs. When he is free, he moves quickly to* **Esther**. *Unrestricted they kiss violently, with a great and private passion, as if they've forgotten that they're being watched. Their clothes are twisted out of shape by the embrace, lipstick smeared across* **Jakob**'s *face. Eventually they release each other, remember where they are.* **Jakob** *smoothes a hand through his hair.* **Esther** *tries to straighten her skirt. Seeing* **Cranmer** *watching her, she starts suddenly to cry.*

Esther   You want to humiliate me, is that it, Mr Cranmer, you want for me to feel a whore for touching my husband?

Cranmer   No. I wanted for you to remember a little what it means to be alive, remember that you're not dead, not yet.

Jakob *puts his hands to his wife's cheek.*

Jakob   It's OK, Esther. It's OK . . . Mr Cranmer, thank you.

Cranmer (*surprised*)   Let's sit and talk a little.

Esther *sits.* **Jakob** *stays standing.*

Cranmer   You look different now, Jakob. Two years in the Death House. You look worn down.

Jakob   Why are you here, Mr Cranmer?

Cranmer   To save your life.

Jakob (*tired*)   You're the one that's gonna save my life, Mr Cranmer? That's what keeps you up at nights, knowing you're that guy?

Cranmer   In ten days you will be executed. There are appeals and they will fail and in ten days you will be executed.

Pause.

Jakob   Yes.

Cranmer   Save yourself. Save your wife. Save your family. Tell the truth.

Esther   We have told the truth. We are innocent. We will be murdered by the government of the United States.

Cranmer   I know what you did. We all know what you did.

Jakob   Tell that to the crowds on the streets. To the newspaper editors. To the people writing the plays. Tell that to the world that knows, that damn well knows, you are destroying an innocent family.

Cranmer   You want to know what you're gonna martyr yourself to?

Jakob   I know what it is.

Cranmer   You will be a martyr to murderers and gangsters. You think Russia's the Holy Land? Stalin picked his teeth on the graves of the workers. Millions of graves.

Jakob   I don't believe you.

Cranmer   We think maybe fifteen million dead peasants, in the '30s. Prison camps in Siberia. Man-made famine in the Ukraine, seven, maybe eight million dead there. You know why the Nazis got to the gates of Moscow in the first place? Because Uncle Joe had killed half his army before the Fascists even started looking East.

Jakob   I don't believe you.

Cranmer   I know. I have documents.

Jakob   I don't want to see them.

Cranmer   Look.

He puts a document wallet on the table. **Jakob** *doesn't open it.*

Jakob   You think you are my friend, Mr Cranmer, you think you become my friend showing me this?

Cranmer   I'm not asking you to save yourself for yourself, but to do it for the people who will end up in those graves. If you go through with this you're not protecting your own little lies, you're dying –

Esther   We have the courage because of our convictions –

Cranmer   – you're dying for the big lies, and that is a crime of example –

Jakob   Whatever you say about the Soviet Union, you don't see it, Mr Cranmer, do you? It is the duty of all righteous men to fight undeserved privilege and it is a fight with no end. There's no document you can offer with words bigger than that.

Cranmer   Still think of yourself as a believer, Jakob, is that it? Think you're like a kamikaze, a suicide pilot?

Jakob (*with great feeling*)   That revolution was an idea. The most beautiful idea in the world. You think you're bigger than that? Nothing is bigger than that. It's dignity. It's the rock sung in the Psalms and if you think you can take that from us you are wrong.

Cranmer   The rock sung in the Psalms?

Jakob (*passionate*)   Yes. Yes. Yes.

Pause.

Cranmer   You know, when I came back from Germany, after the war, I drove out to my father's house. We sat quietly and drank a beer and I wanted to feel like a man. But, you know, there was something I wanted to ask him. You see, my father, he'd come back twenty-five years earlier, come back from the first war. I wanted to ask him why he never spoke about it. Wanted to ask him why he'd never been proud of what he'd done. You know what he said when I asked him?

Jakob   No.

Cranmer   He said, 'Every war isn't a crusade.' But you think we live in the time of crusades, don't you? In the times of crisis you choose, right Jakob, you choose which side you're on. What you believe in.

Jakob   You choose, yeah.

Cranmer   But you understand there's no miracle here, Jakob. No miraculous ascension. Just the chair. Just the death room and the burning.

Pause.

Jakob   I remember my father. He died just after the war. I remember sitting with him, when he was real sick, in his little room in his little place. The room he was going to die in. And we just talked a little. He was so separate those days, so far away, and I didn't have words for how I admired him. Once you know you're going, it's different. Everything's different. You told me you want for me to think that I'm still alive. But I'm not. This is my life after I died. You're not yourself once you're dead. You're your admirers'. You're what they think of you. (*Flip.*) You're history.

Pause.

Esther   Mr Cranmer, I've missed my recordings. I liked to listen to them, loud, when the apartment was empty. The way the voices mixed together as they sang, got louder all together, I liked that. All the journalists that write about us, about what you're doing to us, the radio broadcasts and the marches in the streets, all the people that know we are innocent, that you want to murder us, they're the voices, mingled together, getting louder, you understand that?

Cranmer   Yes.

Esther   Can I ask you something?

Cranmer   Sure.

Esther   How come it's you?

Cranmer   What do you mean?

Esther   Here. Now. Making me this offer of my life. How come it's you? If Hoover doesn't trust you?

Cranmer   The meeting was arranged through back channels.

Esther   Back channels?

Cranmer   Yeah.

Esther   So Hoover doesn't know about this?

Cranmer   No.

Esther   I don't believe you. I don't believe in what you say you can do.

Cranmer (*angry now*)   For God's sake, Esther, let me help you. Confess and live. For your own sake. For the sake of your son.

Esther   Don't talk to me about my son.

Cranmer   You're gonna orphan your son for an idea.

Jakob Our ideas are more important than our lives. Our ideas outlive us.

Pause.

Cranmer
'Lord, how long will thou look on?
Rescue my soul from their destructions,
My darling from the lions.'

I know the psalms too, Jakob. I had a little book. To fit in a pocket. When I was in Europe. You save them. Save your darlings from the lions. That's all I ask.

Jakob You don't know who they are.

Cranmer You know. You choose. You decide. I'll be back in ten minutes.

He leaves.

A long silence.

Jakob *and* **Esther** *look at each other, trying to decide.*

Jakob You know I always liked that about you?

Esther (*gently*) What?

Jakob That movement. You just did it.

Esther Did what?

Jakob When you think about something, kinda consider something, you move the back of your hand to just directly before your lips. I always liked it when you did that.

Esther You did?

Jakob Thought it was beautiful, grown-up but still like a kid too. Tried to copy it, but I never could. Tried to copy your gestures all the time, all through our marriage, tried to learn you.

Esther I could remember you, too. Every day in here I remembered every little thing.

Jakob   Yeah?

They are crying openly.

Esther   My husband. My son.

Jakob   Am I a selfish man?

Esther   No.

Jakob   I am a selfish man.

Esther   Why?

Jakob (*with agonised shame*)   Because maybe I want to live. Because now, in this room, I want to deny the man that I have spent my life trying to become. Because maybe I want to live, because I want my wife to live. Every night, when the lights go out and I hear the guards come past the door of my cell, I have to tense my body against itself, because I would go down on my knees in front of that man and confess all the sins of my life, like a child, just so that I could be saved from being the man that I have tried to become.

Esther (*going to her husband*)   It's what we let them take away.

Jakob   What do you mean?

Esther   They want us to be liars. They want us to be nothing, for us to be a dirty word.

Jakob   Everything I've done to you, I'm sorry –

Esther   You have done nothing to me –

Jakob   I could save you if I give them what they want –

Esther   I don't need that, Jakob, I don't need that.

Pause.

Once you told us all about the people that rebelled in the camps, the ones that were slaughtered. The nameless people, the ones only known by the wind and the smoke. You tried to explain it to, to Doovey, and you said 'Sometimes the gesture matters.' Cranmer and those people, they think we're not big enough inside, they think we're not enough, that a gesture's too big for people like us.

Jakob   Those dead people, the ones who fought back, they knew what would happen but they did it still. They did it still.

Esther   Yeah.

Pause.

There was this girl at high school. A plain girl, girl nobody looked much at. But I remember after a vacation she came back different. Yeah, she'd changed her hair or her dress, I don't know, but it was something else. She had decided to be remarked upon, to be more than a plain girl. She realised she could be more and how to do it and so she was. Some days we choose who we're gonna be.

Jakob   And you've chosen?

Esther   Yes.

Jakob   Yes. Me too. A long time ago, I don't remember when.

He kisses his wife.

What do we do about Cranmer?

Esther   The press. Tell the press he offered us our lives in order to lie for him.

Pause. **Jakob** *uneasy about this new lie.*

Jakob   Yeah, we could do that.

Scene Two

1975.

Matthew's *apartment.*

The wooden table is covered in books and documents, dozens of newspapers and the fragments of a speech in **Matthew**'s *handwriting on various scattered sheets. Music, loud, comes from the record player: Sam Cooke, singing 'Nobody Knows the Trouble I've Seen'.* **Matthew** *stands in front of the table, a pen in one hand, moving within the music. He is happy.*

There is a knock at the door. **Matthew** *makes no effort to turn down the music.*

Matthew It's open.

No one enters.

Hey, it's open.

Anna *enters, looking pale and wearing a sweater that's too big for her, something she can hug herself in. They watch each other for a moment and then* **Matthew** *moves towards the record player, turns off the music. They stand apart.*

Silence.

Matthew So. Kissing cousins.

Anna Yeah.

Matthew It was in the papers, I saw it there. 'Girshfeld daughter in suicide attempt.' There was a college picture. Someone cut it out for me. Got my attention.

Anna My father found me. Took me to the hospital. A guy at the hospital recognised him and called the papers, that's all.

Pause.

Matthew Why didn't you come talk to me?

Anna What do you mean?

Matthew   To say goodbye at least –

Anna   What I did, it wasn't 'cause of you –

Matthew   I could have helped you, I think.

Anna   I just didn't feel I could. Didn't feel it was the right thing to do.

Matthew   You'd have left with no goodbye.

Anna   Changed my mind halfway through. There was no danger.

Matthew   Why did you come here?

Anna   For you.

Matthew   What do you mean?

Beat.

Anna   Please. Let me speak.

Matthew (*gently*)   Come in.

Anna *enters the room. They keep apart from each other.*

Anna   Tomorrow you do the press conference? Tomorrow is the Rubenstein Rally?

Matthew   Yes.

Anna   Make your speech for the cameras about their innocence?

Matthew   About their innocence yeah.

Anna (*fact*)   Make that statement for all time.

Matthew   Yeah.

Pause.

Anna   Matthew, I went to my father, which I haven't done for a long time. I went to my father and whatever else he did wrong, when he said they gave the bomb away he told the truth. I saw it in his eyes.

Matthew   You came here to tell me that?

Anna   Matthew –

Matthew   Don't talk to me about David Girshfeld, don't talk to me about your father. Your father disgusts me. I have defined my life by not being your father.

Anna   But so have I – don't you see, Matthew, so have I.

Matthew   If you want to protect him, you do that, but don't talk to me about his honesty –

Anna   I never wanted to protect him, I wanted to hurt him, I went to that house so that I could punish him, so that I could die in front of him. I never even wrote a note because I was the note –

Matthew   – a gesture –

Anna   – yeah, a gesture . . . (*Her feeling rising.*) I had to change my name too, Matthew. Because we were hated. Not pitied, like you, hated. My father's not Doovey any more. Not for a long time. He's a man who can't sleep through the night.

Matthew   You think I care about that?

Anna (*with anguish*)   They died because I was born. Because of me. In my head that's what it is, they died because my father wanted to protect me. When I was a child I woke up from dreams of a man strapped in a chair with his head on fire. And I couldn't even tell my parents about those dreams. So I needed to know the truth like you need to know the colour of your own eyes, like you need to know your age or the day you were born on, because I needed to know what sort of person I was. Because I felt the guilt of being alive when other people were dead.

Matthew (*he understands*)   I know.

Anna   What you're looking for, you won't find it.

Matthew   I've already found it, Anna. When I read those documents it was like entering a room they'd just left. The coffee cooling in the cup. And you can't know what that is to me, that connection. Tomorrow I'm gonna make a speech about my parents, about what is true, a speech that will set the fucking building on fire.

Pause.

Anna   You know what? I was going to say, 'Hey, Mickey Mouse,' say it kinda understated.

Matthew   What?

Anna   When I came in just now. I thought I should plan a thing to say. In case it was tense.

Matthew (*amused*)   Oh, you guessed it might be a little tense?

Anna   Yeah.

Matthew   Yeah.

Anna   Not a great opening though. Mickey Mouse.

Matthew   I don't know. I think that's pretty good.

Pause.

You really didn't know who I was? When we met?

Anna   No. You know me?

Matthew   Not an idea.

Anna   Not an idea?

Matthew   No.

Anna   It's more than that. I'd never have looked for you. Never. I never wanted to see you, you ever guess that? My whole life. Rather have seen any person in the world than you. I mean the real you. When I was a little girl I had this fear that I'd go to school one day and find you transferred to my class, to my school, and you telling the other kids what had been done to you, and everyone knowing, knowing what I'd done.

Matthew   You didn't do anything to me, Anna.

Anna   No?

Matthew   You know what? I honestly never gave you a thought. Your father, seeing him, yeah, maybe I thought and dreamt about that, but you? No. You had no life for me.

Anna (*moved*)   I'd never have thought that.

Matthew   You're scared to be here, I can see that. But what you gave me, what you made me remember about myself, about my family, it's precious to me.

Anna   I know that. I've been thinking why was it we liked each other. More than just strange recognition.

Matthew   Why?

Anna   Need. That's what we inherit. The constitution we get from our parents. Not cells and blood, but a type of need. Our habits of loving, the kind of other people we need to make us whole.

Matthew   Anna, you understand I can't do what you want me to do. Tomorrow. Tomorrow I have to do what is right. What I believe.

Anna   Whatever you say tomorrow it doesn't matter to me any more. I care for you. I just don't want to see you hurt. And I think that you will be. I came to you today to say that maybe we don't have to live like this any more, don't have to live with the past like razor blades inside us.

They become aware of someone at the door, perhaps a knock at the open door.

Paul Cranmer, *sixty years old, stands at the door with a battered briefcase in his hands.*

Cranmer   Matthew Maddison?

Matthew   Matthew Rubenstein.

Cranmer   May I come in?

Matthew   Who are you?

Cranmer   Paul Cranmer.

Matthew   Don't know who you are.

Cranmer (*remembering the past*)   FBI.

Matthew   I have nothing to say to the FBI.

Cranmer   I'm retired.

Matthew   It doesn't matter to me.

Cranmer   In 1951 I arrested your father. It was me that did that.

Beat.

Matthew (*he is calm*)   What do you want, Mr Cranmer?

Anna   Leave. Please leave. I know why he's here, Matthew –

Matthew   You murdered my parents, what do you want here?

Cranmer   I'm here to give you something, Matthew. To give you the truth.

Matthew   What does the FBI know about the truth?

Cranmer   We knew everything, even then –

Anna   Make him leave, Matthew I know who he is –

Matthew   Nothing you could say would ever make a difference to me, you understand that, Mr Cranmer?

Cranmer   Then you are like your father.

Matthew   Yes, I am. What his example taught me to be.

Cranmer   I hope you understand, when I'm gone, that I only came to stop the waste of your life, to stop you being what your father taught you to be.

Anna   Leave him alone. Please. Leave Matthew alone.

Cranmer (*with feeling*)   No, it's that . . . your father told me something once and I believed in it. I think of it often. I believed it but I never found a way to do it. To serve it. I didn't do it.

Matthew *looks at* **Cranmer**, *lets him into the room.*

Matthew   What do you want to say?

Anna   Don't listen to him, Matthew, don't listen to any more haunted old men. That's what I came to say –

Cranmer (*to* **Anna**)   You want to know what really haunted me? What they gave away, the information, it was kinda skimpy, a thing the Russians had already got somewhere else. It was finding that out that changed my mind, in the end. (*Beat.*) It should be just for you, Matthew, not your girlfriend.

Matthew (*looks at* **Anna**)   No, really, she should stay.

Cranmer (*doesn't know who she is.*)   OK.

He opens his briefcase, takes out an old thick folder.

What I'm going to give you, it's just to help you. What you do tomorrow, what happens to the Bureau after tomorrow, I don't care. (*He puts the folder onto the wooden table.*) In 1943, in the middle of World War Two, US Intelligence began an operation to intercept and break coded messages sent between Moscow and Soviet embassies in the West. The operation was called Venona. I don't know why. By 1945 they had decrypted two hundred thousand Soviet messages. By 1946 they had begun to expose the attempts of Soviet intelligence agencies, what we call now the KGB, to penetrate the atomic bomb project at Los Alamos, New Mexico. The decryptions provided details of locations, code-names and the activities of American citizens working for the Soviet Union in the United States. The achievement was so startling and so secret that it was kept from Presidents Roosevelt and Truman.

Matthew *stands by the door.* **Anna** *has retreated to the corner of the room.*

Matthew (*uneasy*)   Why does this matter to me?

Cranmer   Your father's codename was 'Democrat'. David Girshfeld was 'Player'. Esther Rubenstein was 'Nightingale'. In January 1945, Jakob Rubenstein and David Girshfeld delivered sketches of some internal workings of the plutonium bomb to agents of the KGB.

Matthew   You're lying to me. If this was true you'd have told the whole fucking world during the trial.

Cranmer   Venona could never be released to the public. Even the FBI knew the rumours but not the details. When you break a code, you can't do anything to let the enemy know that their communications are being read, because they'll just change the method again. I'm breaking the law, now, at this moment, to tell you this.

Beat.

Your father microfilmed stolen documents at his apartment in Knickerbocker Village. Your father recruited and ran agents for the Russians. The name of your father was known to Stalin, to Khrushchev, to Head of KGB Beria. Your father was a spy. Your father, and others like him, gave the secret of the atomic bomb to the Soviet Union.

Pause.

Anna   You should leave now.

Cranmer   Read. The passages highlighted are the relevant ones. (*He stands. With awkwardness:*)   Matthew . . . your father . . . I didn't come here to ruin things for you, to hurt his son. I came because I liked him.

Matthew   You liked him?

Cranmer   Yeah, it surprised me, but I did.

He moves to leave.

Matthew   Wait. (*Beat.*) What were they like?

Cranmer   What?

Matthew (*something childlike*)   My parents. What were they like?

Cranmer (*he doesn't expect this*)   I . . . your mother I hardly knew.

Matthew   My father?

Cranmer   I think he believed. I think so. I think he lived in a world of believers, who fought. Men like that, they change the world or they get destroyed by it.

Matthew   But you liked him.

Cranmer   Yeah, I did. This is my gift to your father: don't waste your life for a pretence.

Matthew   I'm not doing that.

Cranmer (*thinking of* **Jakob**)   You know my son got a new camera. It has a timer on it, which lets you frame a photograph, and then run to get into the frame you've set. I was with him last week and he took a picture. A portrait. My son and his wife, me and my wife. That's what the past is, running into the picture after you've set the timer. Being seen how you want to be seen. The breath held in to hold the smile.

Read Venona. I'll leave it here for an hour. Read it or not. But the truth is in there. What you said you wanted is in there. You choose.

He leaves.

Matthew *sits on the floor. After a moment* **Anna** *moves to the table, to the folder.*

Anna   You don't have to look at this, Matthew. You don't have to ever open it.

Matthew   No.

Anna   Let's just go out, get out of this room, let's just go and get coffee and forget and live.

Matthew *looks at her for a long moment. He decides.*

Matthew   Read. You read –

Anna   Matthew, no –

Matthew   Read.

He closes his eyes. **Anna** *opens the folder and begins to read.*

Silence.

Anna   It says that Jakob was recruited in 1942. That he told the Russians he had a brother, who was a machinist, who was going to be working for the army. That his brother was at that point a single man.

Matthew   Your father could have told them that. Go on. Read more.

Anna *(reluctant)*   OK.

She flicks through the pages of the folder.

Jakob's Soviet contact was Valentin Geller –

Matthew   No, go on –

Anna   'Democrat' was advised to leave the party in 1942 in order to reduce his visibility to the FBI –

Matthew   No, that means nothing –

Anna   A sphere of uranium from Los Alamos was presented to KGB officers in Washington by Jakob Rubenstein in January 1945 –

Matthew   No, they couldn't even prove that at the trial. More.

Anna *(reading on)*   Oh Jesus, Matthew, maybe this is all bullshit.

Matthew *(hope)*   Is it?

Anna   I think so, maybe. Look, it says here that in 1943 the Rubensteins 'were given instructions on how to alter household furniture to allow the concealment of espionage materials. To contain photographic equipment and documents.' I mean, that's made up. Come on. It's James Bond.

Matthew   What did you say?

Anna   It's like a movie, I mean.

Matthew   Household furniture?

Anna   Yeah, like a chair or a night-stand, I guess –

Matthew *stands and looks at* **Anna** *with growing knowledge. He walks around the wooden table, his attention focused on it. He moves towards it, runs his hands over its surfaces.*

Matthew   She kept the table. The table, my grandmother kept the table.

He upends the table, sending his papers and trial transcripts flying onto the floor. He kneels next to the table, its legs in the air. He traces his hand over the wood on its under-surface. Near one of the legs, in the join between the leg and the underside of the table surface he finds a small, chiselled opening. He pushes his hand into it. It is empty.
Matthew *shows the gap, pulls his hand out of it.* **Anna** *pushes her hand into it. They sit side by side, next to the table. They are silent.*

Matthew   They did it. They did it.

Anna *moves towards him, but he pushes her away.*

Anna   Matthew, my sweet Matthew, it means nothing, nothing –

Matthew   It means everything – my parents, they lied. They lied. I was sure of them and they lied; all my life, they lied, how can I be a person when I know that – they were everything that meant anything to me, and I am a man who could do anything now because they lied, they left me this thing, they left me for a lie –

Scene Three

The action in the scene is split between the two periods: New York, 1975 – **Matthew***'s apartment, on the morning of the Rubenstein Rally; and June 1953 – the Death House, Sing Sing Prison, on the day of execution.*

Lights up on 1975.

The wooden table has been put back, and is bare of papers. **Matthew** *sits at the table. He is wearing a suit for the first time in the play.* **Anna** *sits in the corner of the room, watching him. They have not spoken for many minutes.*

Matthew   I used to talk to him here, you know.

Anna   You did?

Matthew   Sitting at the table. It was like a relic, like a thing in a religion, because I knew he had touched it.

Pause.

I sat here last night. After you went home. Tried to talk here again. But it was like a phone line went dead . . . I never thought that would happen. I thought when you loved something there was no cutting-off point, no past and present, just a mingling together, a kinda . . . concurrency, heh, is that a word?

Anna   Concurrency?

Matthew   Yeah.

Anna (*smiles*)   I don't think so.

Matthew   It should be.

Pause.

Anna   Matthew, what will you do?

Matthew   Today, you mean?

Anna   Yeah.

Matthew   What speech will I make at the Rubenstein Rally? What will I tell all the people come to hear the heir speak out?

Anna   Matthew, listen to me. You understand that we can come through this good? Do you see that chance? You understand that I love you for you now, that there's truth in that, hope in that, family in that. That there can be a positive thing in all of this. Purpose in this. Reason in this. You are my cousin. I know you now. You are my blood. And they . . . they were my uncle and my aunt. You understand me? Connected. When you love someone, sometimes things change, what you know changes, but still when you really love someone there's no past and there's no present.

Pause.

Matthew   I don't know . . . Hey, answer me one thing. If you have to make a choice, who do you betray? Is there a place I can go and find that out?

Lights down on 1975.

Lights up on 1953. **Jakob** *and* **Esther** *sit, without cuffs, on opposite sides of an iron-mesh screen.*

They have not spoken for many minutes. **Jakob** *is agitated.*

Jakob   Did you sleep last night?

Esther   I slept a little.

Jakob   I always wondered about that, through these years. What I'd do. Seemed sorta blasphemous to sleep through your last night. Not to cherish it.

Esther   Didn't you sleep, darling man?

Jakob   Not one moment.

Pause.

You know what I always hated?

Esther   What?

Jakob   Things, that they're always over too soon.

Pause.

I can't say to you that I'm not scared. I can't say that.

Esther   No.

Jakob   Are you scared?

Esther   It's strange, but I don't think I am.

Pause.

Jakob (*becoming increasingly agitated*)   It's not the big things in my head now. It's the . . . the . . . procedure. I mean, last night I wanted to spend thinking about the things in my life but I kept finding myself just thinking about the procedure. It's the straps – I can't think of the straps on the arms and then the hood over the eyes, that dark moment before they throw the switch. I just don't know how people thought to do that to other people –

Esther   Jakob –

Jakob   – and I didn't know why they had to put you in the dark before they put you in the dark and then some warden told me it's because your . . . your eyes, they burst like eggs running down your face –

Esther   Stay with me, Jakob –

Jakob   How do they think to do that to a person – ?

Esther   Help me, stay with me, help me –

Jakob   Help you?

Esther   Help me with this. Help me with what we write for Matthew.

Pause

Jakob   I have this feeling that people are watching us and saying Jakob is falling apart, like we sorta guessed he was gonna, cause she was always the strong one.

Esther   People don't know nothing about us.

Jakob   No.

Pause.

Esther (*reminding him*)   Matthew.

Jakob   Yeah.

Lights up on 1975. Lights remain on 1953.

Anna   I can't tell you what to do.

Matthew   I know.

Esther   What we write now, Jakob, what we say, it will matter.

Jakob   Yes.

Esther   What we want our son to think, what the people who come after think.

Jakob (*with anger*)   And that's the worst thing, the not knowing how things will end, what will happen after we are dead, who will win this war.

Esther   This is how we help what should happen, happen.

Matthew   What I wanted, before I even got into this, all I wanted was for them to be proud of me. To be worthy of what was given, what was handed down.

Anna   Ask yourself how you do that.

Jakob (*with feeling*)   Write this: 'Never forget that we were innocent. Never forget that we died because certain things have to be protected.'

Matthew   We must protect the people who need to be protected.

Jakob   'When you are older you will understand that sometimes people are chosen to fight certain battles, and even if they don't want that, it is their responsibility. This was our responsibility.'

Matthew   Whatever I wanted, I was responsible to them, for them.

Anna   But if maybe you just tell the truth, what you know of the truth, if you just say that what they did, what all of them did, was just what any person could have done then everybody would understand, it would be real to everybody.

Esther   'We were innocent and could not give up our lives in the support of a lie.'

Matthew   You think, like Cranmer thinks, I can just leave this now? Just give it up? I don't think people can be like that. I think the war is transmitted to us, in our fucking cells, down the generations, like a virus, in our blood like holy wine, and there's nothing we can do to stop that.

Anna   Maybe. But maybe that's what's wrong with us. We could go there, today, go there together. We're big enough to do that. We could break the cycle. This is what we should do, what I think we should do. Tell the truth and forgive and live on.

Esther   I can't leave my son just this. Just this memory.

Matthew   They knew what would happen, and they still died like that, made that choice and after all this time and all these words I still don't know why they did what they did. How they faced it.

Anna   They died for vanity, Matthew. You can't give your name to that lie.

Matthew   That's not what I'll be doing. That's not what I'm giving my name to.

Esther   'But whatever you do, never forget that we loved you and that life is worth loving and it is worth living for its own sake.'

Anna   So what will you do?

Beat.

Matthew   Fight. Carry it on. Make a speech. Fight.

Anna   If you do that, it'll never end.

Matthew   It won't ever end.

He stands, buttons his jacket. Lights down on 1975.

Lights left on 1953. **Jakob** *is calmer.* **Esther** *holds the letter in her hands.*

Esther   I wish they could have let us have a room with no metal screen. Just for today.

Jakob (*smiles*)   I would have liked that.

Esther (*smiling too*)   I know. To hold you in my body, just one time again.

Jakob (*blushes*)   Yeah.

Esther   Embarrassed?

Jakob   A little bit, yeah.

Esther   My strange man.

Pause.

That would have been a nice thing they could have done.

Pause.

Jakob   Here. Put your finger through here.

He forces his finger through one of the small gaps in the wire mesh. It is a difficult thing to do, painful. **Esther** *takes his finger in one of hers.*

Jakob   Can you feel?

Esther   Yeah. I feel like a kid, like we're gonna get caught.

Jakob   Yeah.

They hold each other's fingers.

Answer me this. Have I been a good husband?

Esther   Yes.

Jakob   Really?

Esther   The best.

Jakob   I'm sorry that I didn't protect you better.

Pause. His finger is bleeding from the wire.

Jesus. I'm bleeding.

Esther   Yes.

Jakob   I guess it don't matter so much today.

Esther   No.

She neels and leans forward with great grace. She takes the tiny available part of his finger in her mouth.

Your blood. I can taste it. It's in me.

Jakob   I love you.

Esther   I love you.

Pause.

Jakob   It'll be time soon.

Esther   Yes.

Light fades on 1953.

Lights up on 1975.

It is later that night. **Matthew** *is in shirtsleeves, his tie unknotted.* **Matthew** *and* **Anna** *are about to eat.*

Anna   You made the speech?

Matthew   Yeah. I raised the roof off the building. I did what I said I'd do.

Anna (*with strange acceptance*)   Yeah.

Matthew   It was like nothing that's happened to me. Before, if anybody spoke about my parents, tried to change stuff, it was impossible, it was like despair, like a mute talking to the deaf. But today it was like – Jesus, like inspiration, these people listening, and believing. Nearly felt pure too, nearly, like singing a song under a clear sky.

Anna   So it doesn't end.

Matthew   No.

He stands by the record player.

I want you to listen to this. This is my favourite bit of my mother's favourite opera. Not a famous bit.

Anna   OK.

Matthew *puts the record on. It's the 'Humming Chorus' from* Madam Butterfly. *It begins to play.*

Now the stage is divided into two sections of light, centred along the centre line of the wooden table. In one half of the room we are in the Rubenstein apartment and it is 1942 once again. In the other we are still where we have been, with **Anna** *and* **Matthew** *in 1975.*

In 1942 **Jakob** *is washing his hands and* **Esther** *is finishing preparing their evening meal.*

Esther   So I meant to tell you, tomorrow night Doovey's bringing his new girl over.

Jakob   Tomorrow night?

Esther   He's serious about her.

Jakob   Yeah? How serious?

Esther   Real serious.

Jakob   That's great to hear.

Esther   They'll marry, that's what I think.

Jakob   Your parents happy about that?

Esther   I think so, yeah.

Jakob   Good.

Esther   He'll want your approval.

Jakob (*touched*)   I like that. I like that he wants that.

Esther   He looks up to you, Jakob. (*Smiling.*) He thinks you hung the moon.

Jakob   I know.

Matthew *has put on the record.*

Matthew   It's just these voices, singing together. All these voices singing without words, indistinct, heard over the crest of a hill. I liked that.

And now **Matthew** *and* **Anna** *prepare to eat their meal. In the other section of light, at the other end of the table,* **Jakob** *and* **Esther** *are ready to eat. The two rooms are coming fully together, and it is a busy, domestic picture. Food is placed on the table at different points, mirrored between past and present. There is bread in the middle of the table,* **Esther** *slices it and turns back to her husband.* **Anna** *takes some of the cut bread, puts it on her plate and on* **Matthew***'s.* **Jakob** *fills his glass with juice from a jug which* **Anna** *had placed earlier. In 1942 and 1975* **Jakob** *and* **Matthew** *and* **Esther** *and* **Anna** *sit down at the table. The 'Humming Chorus' fills the theatre. The family eat.*

Printed in the USA
CPSIA information can be obtained
at www.ICGtesting.com
LVHW041059171024
794057LV00001B/157